SOUPS
for the
PROFESSIONAL
CHEF

SOUPS

❧ for the ❧
PROFESSIONAL
❧ CHEF ❧

Terence Janericco

 VAN NOSTRAND REINHOLD COMPANY
_____ New York

641.8
Jan

Printed in the United States of America

Designed by Kathryn Parise

Van Nostrand Reinhold Company Inc.
115 Fifth Avenue
New York, New York 10003

Van Nostrand Reinhold Company Limited
Molly Millars Lane
Wokingham, Berkshire RG11 2PY, England

Van Nostrand Reinhold
480 La Trobe Street
Melbourne, Victoria 3000, Australia

Macmillan of Canada
Division of Canada Publishing Corporation
164 Commander Boulevard
Agincourt, Ontario M1S 3C7, Canada

16 15 14 13 12 11 10 9 8 7 6 5 4 3 2 1

Library of Congress Cataloging-in-Publication Data

Janericco, Terence.
   Soups for the professional chef.

   Includes index.
   1. Soups. I. Title.
TX757.J364   1988   641.8'13   87-29821
ISBN 0-442-24398-7

To Glenna Bradley
For years of loving friendship and continuing support

❧ CONTENTS ❧

❧ PREFACE ❧

The relationship between restaurants and soups goes back to the very beginning of public dining. In prerevolutionary France, the guild in charge of hostels made arrangements to sell soup as a "restorative" to weary travelers. Prior to that one could sleep in an inn but would have to go to a foodshop to get something to eat. Innkeepers realized the wisdom of adding menus first with soups and then with the addition of braised dishes. Thus the modern restaurant began.

Soups have long been a *raison d'être* for restaurants. Many restaurants have made their reputation on soups, and over the years there have been several successful restaurants that served little more than soups and breads. These are now often accompanied by sandwiches or salads to help expand the appeal, but the focal point remains the soup itself.

Soup has always been among the most heartwarming of foods. It can come anywhere in a menu—as a first course, main meal, or dessert. Soup pleases virtually everyone. There are those who announce that they do not like soup, but then they readily approach a chowder or other heartier version. Usually those who claim not to like soup do so because the soups they have been exposed to were watery and flavorless.

Today's professional chefs have more reason than ever to produce soups on a regular basis. There is great interest in fresh ingredients and in foods that are free of chemical additives—the very virtues of homemade soups. With a minimum amount of effort the professional chef can produce an exciting, delicious first course to entice the diner into the main course—and also to help increase sales. People who might think twice about having a hearty first course will succumb to a wonderful cup of soup. The Zodiac Rooms at

Neiman-Marcus department stores have long had the custom of serving a cup of chicken broth to customers as soon as they sit down. This is so relaxing after an arduous morning of shopping that customers immediately feel restored and think about ordering "luncheon" rather than a quick sandwich. Again, with the interest in lighter foods, a soup can receive a far better acceptance than the more customary offering of relishes or a cheese tray.

Of course, another advantage of soups is that they can be prepared inexpensively. The clever soup chef learns to get flavor out of all sorts of ingredients, even those that might otherwise be discarded. Carrot tops, onion stems, celery leaves, and the like can be used to prepare flavorful stocks and from those, delicious soups. Chefs in charge of larger kitchens where butchering is done on the premises have a supply of beef and veal bones to use in making rich stocks. Fish restaurants have the ingredients readily available to make an inexpensive but truly delicious fish soup for what amounts to pennies a serving. Turning lobster bodies and shrimp shells into creamy bisques does take a little time, but the food cost is negligible and the appeal to diners is enormous. And the soup that does not sell out on one day will often sell the next without loss of quality. Or it can serve as the base for yet another soup.

Regrettably, many restaurants and hotel kitchens produce less than pleasing soups. Laziness, or perhaps a lack of education in cookery, causes too many chefs to resort to serving canned soups rather than making their own. Too many kitchens use jars of bouillon mix in making stock rather than making a real stock with the bones of meat, poultry, or fish. At one time the public expected and accepted soups of this ilk, but now clients are more aware of fresh food and less willing to accept the off flavors of canned soups and stock bases.

Those chefs who think their customers will not notice should give their customers more credit. Can anyone other than a food manufacturer's commissary possibly produce the particular texture, shape, and color of a canned mushroom? There is certainly no resemblance to a real mushroom, and the customer knows it. Every day the public is demanding more quality for its dollar. People will spend large sums of money to dine well, but no longer will they spend money on canned food. Customers want variety and freshness and they will seldom settle for less. As any experienced restaurateur knows, it is not the customer who creates a scene that we must worry about; he can probably be appeased. Rather, it is the customer who silently leaves—never to return—who is the concern.

Today every chef should be able to prepare a host of wonderful soups. They are easy—usually without cause for concern. Generally, the soup can be prepared well in advance and will just improve if left over low heat for long periods. In addition, for a small food cost you can create a reputation for honest food that will have customers vying for a place at your table.

𝕰 EQUIPMENT AND 𝕰 STORAGE

Most professional kitchens have the equipment required for preparing soups. However, certain pieces of equipment work better than others. The finish of a soup—how it feels on the tongue—changes according to the equipment used. Therefore, you will notice that I sometimes recommend using hand equipment over machines because of the superior result. To give an example, in making a velouté, that is, an absolutely velvety soup as smooth as silk, the best result is achieved by forcing it through the finest blade of a food mill *several* times and then through fine strainers. This effort results in a mouthful of flavor without texture, the way the soup ought to be. If you are inclined to use a food processor you will get a fine soup, but the texture will be wrong. The food mill removes all of the fibrous parts of the vegetables and forces all the flavor from them into the soup, whereas the processor chops the vegetables very finely but incorporates the fibrous parts into the soup.

KETTLES

Obviously, every kitchen should have large kettles or stockpots. And in soup cookery, the choice of pot is especially important. Aluminum pots work well for most soups. They should not be used, however, for soups that have a fair amount of acidic ingredients, such as soups made with tomatoes. In this case, a soup that ought to have been delicious will instead have a metallic and often bitter taste. Nor should you use aluminum pots in making cream soups. The steady stirring required when creating the liaison of soup base,

1

cream, and egg yolks can result in a soup of a gray, dingy-looking color rather than a delicate cream color.

Unquestionably, the best pots for soup cookery are those made of tin- or steel-lined copper. They can be very expensive, however, and the cost may not be justified. Their principal advantage is that they provide even heat and the lining will not affect the flavor of the soups. Nickel linings are not recommended because the lining wears out so quickly and is not only very difficult to replace but also expensive.

Stainless-steel pots cost a little more than aluminum and a little less than copper. The steel will not give off any metallic flavor and the metal will not turn the soups gray. Steel is a poor conductor of heat, however, which means that thick soups, especially cream soups, can burn more readily in a steel pot than in one made of copper or aluminum. When purchasing a stainless-steel pot, make sure the bottom is very heavy, preferably composed of a sandwich of steel and another metal such as copper or aluminum. Check the sides of the pot to make sure they too are thick. Often steel pots are made with a thick base and very thin sides. Because of the poor heat conduction, the soup or other food can burn along the sides even though the bottom is cooking evenly. And, of course, burned food will taste burned whether the charring happens on the bottom or on the sides of the pot.

In recent years manufacturers have developed a new type of material that is in fact virtually perfect for soup making. It is sold under several brand names: Calphalon and T-FA1 are two examples.

The base is a good heavy-weight aluminum pot that is covered with a particularly strong gray coating that is impervious to food acids and does not wear off when a soup calls for a lot of stirring. The pots are sturdy and stand up to rough treatment without needing to be relined, as does copper. The cost is similar to that of copper or stainless steel, but worth it.

The ideal kitchen will have pots of a variety of materials for preparing various soups. Large aluminum or stainless-steel pots can be used to make stocks that do not include tomatoes or other acidic foods. Remember, if the liquid is mostly water and the resulting essence of the food, then burning of the soup is not likely, because there is nothing to burn. There are exceptions, of course, such as those stocks made with gelatinous bones. When the gelatin has dissolved, it becomes a major component of the stock, and because gelatin burns easily, you must be careful to avoid this. When preparing a lobster bisque, use a stainless-steel or tin-lined copper pot to prevent the tomatoes from giving the soup an off flavor. But a bisque is thick, and when using a stainless-steel pot you must take care to see that the soup does not burn. Generally, we recommend that you use large aluminum or steel pots for stocks, and make thick bases or very acidic soups in smaller pots of lined copper. Enameled steel has no place in the professional kitchen; the enameling chips easily and the resulting flakes can be dangerous.

FOOD MILLS, FOOD PROCESSORS, AND BLENDERS

Today no kitchen is complete without one version of a food processor, whether it is a household-type Cuisinart in a small commercial kitchen, a professional Robot Coupe, or a buffalo chopper in a large kitchen. These machines are a great help in preparing many soups. They cut back on work time, especially in preparing the seasoning vegetables. Later they can be used for pureeing some soups at the end of the cooking time. Their chief shortcoming is in the preparation of delicate cream-of-vegetable soups. The machines chop the vegetables but do not strain out the fibrous parts. Delicate soups need to be strained, and often strained again, to remove the hard parts of the ingredients such as celery strings or the woody centers of leeks. If the vegetables are merely chopped—no matter how fine—they give the soup a coarse finish rather than one of silken smoothness.

A blender can work very well in pureeing many soups and often do a better job than a processor. Again, however, the blender does not strain out the fibrous portions of the foods. This drawback aside, processors and blenders are wonderful machines and should have a place of honor in every well-appointed kitchen. Their uses are manifold.

A food mill, a rather old-fashioned piece of equipment that takes muscle and time to operate, is also invaluable in making silken-smooth soups. I recommend a 3-quart mill with interchangeable blades. The advantage of the food mill over machines is that it not only purees the food, it removes all strings and hard, fibrous parts. If the vegetables are large, start with a large-holed disk and progress to the finest disk. It may still be necessary to strain the soup through a fine-mesh conical strainer (china cap) to achieve the ultimate smoothness.

Sieves in various sizes are extremely important in preparing soups and bisques. After the soup has been put through the finest blade of the food mill, it can still have some fibrous material. Straining it through the china cap should remove even the smallest lumps. (Years ago, fine kitchens took the preparation a step further and forced the soup through sheets of muslin. It does produce a perfect result, but the time and effort may not make it worthwhile.)

Colanders are of course necessary for straining large amounts of stock before turning the stock into soup. Colanders can also serve as a support for cheesecloth or muslin when straining consommés.

STORING AND FREEZING SOUPS

Soups can, of course, be stored overnight in a refrigerator with no ill effect and often with positive results from the melding of the flavors. Most large kitchens make soup daily, or at least every other day. Smaller establishments may find that one day a week is all they need to make the stocks and bases for the rest of the week's soups.

Large hotels with active catering departments may find it to their advantage to prepare soups, soup bases, and stocks ahead of time and keep them in their freezers. This allows them to distribute the work load more evenly and have cooking equipment available for a series of large functions.

Any of the soups here will keep at least three days under refrigeration. If it becomes necessary to keep a base or soup longer than that, I advise that the soup be brought to a full boil and simmered for 15 minutes before it is cooled and refrigerated again. If for any reason you need to keep a soup or base for longer than six days, it should be frozen. Store soup in containers with sealable lids. If you are going to freeze the soup, leave room for expansion.

Soups and stocks can be frozen for a month or longer. Although there is no loss of quality if the soups are frozen, I recommend that you make soups regularly rather than preparing and freezing huge quantities to last over long periods of time. This allows you to collect the ingredients for the soup over a few days' time, rather than having to buy and assemble ingredients in large quantities.

In freezing soups, use containers of a reasonable size for your operation. If yours is a small operation, it makes no sense to use 5-gallon containers. The freezing process causes ingredients to separate. Thus you cannot thaw just a portion of a frozen soup; you have to thaw the entire container so that you will be able to stir and mix the ingredients. If you know that you will need twenty-four portions at a time, then that is the amount to freeze. If you expect to use twelve or thirty-six portions on an average day, then freeze in those quantities. Even the largest operations should freeze in manageable quantities. If the containers are too big, they take too long to thaw and reheat.

Although most soups freeze easily, there are some dangers to avoid. Freeze cream soup bases without the egg yolk-cream liaison. This should be added shortly before serving, otherwise the soup may curdle when you reheat it. Freezing also affects the texture of some vegetables, carrots for one. Therefore, I recommend that you do not freeze soups containing carrot slices or chunks. Cheese freezes poorly, thus you should prepare only enough cheese soup to be used in a day or so. Generally, meat and fish soups freeze well. Fruit soups can be frozen; however, be careful to add any uncooked liquor only after thawing, since alcohol inhibits freezing.

Ideally, frozen soups should be thawed in a refrigerator overnight. If the soup is not too thick, it can be thawed over direct heat, stirring occasionally.

🦋 BASIC STOCKS 🦋

The foundation of any good kitchen is good stock. Whether you are making soups or not, every professional kitchen should have a generous supply of freshly made stock on hand at all times. It is a necessary ingredient of soups, sauces, and vegetable dishes.

Stock-making does not require a lot of time or effort, and the ingredients can often be salvaged from foodstuffs that would ordinarily be discarded. Once the ingredients are assembled, the stock can be allowed to simmer over low heat for as long as required. Some smaller restaurants put the stock on to cook late at night so that in the morning it will be ready to be strained, defatted, and stored. In larger kitchens there is usually a saucier who makes stock as part of his or her daily activity.

I have found that the cooking times indicated in many older recipes are too long, resulting in a somewhat bitter stock. Fish and poultry stocks do not require hours and hours of cooking time. Generally they are ready in anywhere from thirty minutes to an hour. Chicken stock can be cooked up to two hours; after that I find no improvement in flavor. Of course, if too much liquid has been added to the stock, further cooking may be required to reduce it. I prefer to do that with fresh flavoring ingredients but, if they are not available, a more concentrated stock will itself suffice. Veal and beef stock still require fairly long cooking times, but the simmering requires little or no care on the part of the kitchen staff.

For a stronger stock, cook down the strained stock to enrich its flavor, or let the stock cool, defat it, and use it in place of water in a new preparation.

In a well-run kitchen, the ingredients for stock are essentially free. The thrifty chef will save bones, ends of carrots, celery leaves, onion bases, parsley stems, leek leaves, and other excess bits. When it comes time to make the stock, he or she gathers the ingredients and proceeds. Of course, in many kitchens storage is at a premium and it may be necessary to order bones and meats in order to prepare the stock. Smaller kitchens do not usually butcher their own meat and have no choice but to order it. But even then it may be possible to add many of the vegetable scraps from the day's preparation. Fish bones should be available from your fish supplier at little or no charge. Many poulterers are now charging for backs and necks, however.

It is a waste of money to order the finest vegetables for making stock. Older but flavorful carrots, for example, will do better than the finest young carrots for imparting the carrot essence. Vegetables that are too tired to be used for serving may work wonders in a stock. There is a difference between slightly wilted vegetables and those that are past using, however. Rotten vegetables will produce rotten stock and there will be no savings.

COOKING STOCK

It is necessary to simmer stock gently. Rapid boiling produces a murky and unpalatable stock. Slow, gentle simmering, on the other hand, extracts the flavors from the ingredients and produces a relatively clear, well-flavored stock.

Start all of the ingredients in cold water and bring very slowly to a simmer. If the ingredients have been browned first, it is advisable to let them cool to room temperature before adding the cold water. The cold water allows the flavors to escape into the cooking liquid, giving the stock greater strength. If the stock is started with hot or boiling water, the effect is to seal the flavors within the foods from which you wish to extract them.

After the stock has cooked, gently ladle off the liquid, leaving the solids at the bottom of the pot. If you choose to strain the stock, pour it through a large colander into a large container. Strain it again through a fine sieve or even cheesecloth to remove any small particles. Of course, to achieve a crystal-clear stock, you will need to clarify it. Whether or not to clarify it depends on how you will use the stock. If you are going to use it in cream soups or soups with many ingredients, clarifying is probably unnecessary.

If you intend to make consommé, however, clarifying is not only desirable, it is usually mandatory.

CLARIFYING STOCK

The stock must be cold and should be absolutely free of any fat. With a skimmer scoop the solid fat layer from the surface. If any fat is left and the stock is jelled, use a towel wrung out in hot water to wipe the fat off the surface. If the stock is fluid, drag paper toweling over the surface to pick up any fat globules.

Because the clarifying process removes some flavor, take care not to use more than one egg white for each quart of stock. If, for some reason, it is necessary to repeat the clarifying process, I suggest that you reduce the stock afterwards until the flavor is strong enough.

To clarify stock, place the cold stock, the egg whites, and their shells in a pot. Cook over medium heat, stirring often, until the mixture comes to a boil. Stop stirring immediately, lower the heat, and simmer for at least 10 minutes. Remove from the heat and ladle the stock, including the scum, into a colander lined with several thicknesses of very fine cheesecloth or muslin.

It is extremely important that the mixture be stirred as it comes to a boil so that the coagulated proteins will not drop to the bottom of the pot. Letting it simmer without stirring keeps the proteins in suspension. Take care in ladling the stock into the lined colander that you do not force the stock. Let it drain until only the scum is left. Some chefs prefer to use paper coffee filters instead of cloth to strain the stock, and this works very well. The resulting liquid should be crystal-clear. If it is not, be prepared to repeat the process. If you have used care and attention, however, reclarifying should not be necessary.

Beef Stock

10 pounds beef bones	6 tomatoes, chopped
4 pounds veal bones	6 leeks, chopped
3 carrots, chopped	3 onions, chopped
3 large onions, chopped	3 carrots, chopped
1 quart cold water	4 garlic cloves, chopped
any beef or veal trimmings	15 quarts cold water, approximately
2 to 3 uncooked chicken carcasses	1 tablespoon peppercorns
	3 bay leaves
6 celery stalks and leaves, chopped	1 tablespoon dried thyme
	1 quart cold water
½ bunch parsley, chopped	salt, to taste

Preheat the oven to 450°F.

Cut the bones into 1- to 2-inch pieces and spread them in a roasting pan. Scatter 3 carrots and 3 onions on top, and roast for 1 hour or longer, until the ingredients are well browned but not burned, turning occasionally. Transfer the contents of the roasting pan to a stockpot.

Add 1 quart of cold water to the roasting pan and put it over medium heat. Cook, stirring up the browned bits, until the pan is deglazed. Turn the liquid into the stockpot, and add the beef or veal trimmings, chicken carcasses, celery stalks, parsley, tomatoes, leeks, the remaining carrots and onions, and garlic cloves. Cover with about 15 quarts of cold water and bring slowly to a boil.

Skim off the scum as it rises to the surface. This can take an hour or longer. Continue to remove the scum until it no longer appears. Add the peppercorns, bay leaves, and thyme.

Simmer very gently, uncovered, for 5 to 8 hours, without stirring. Let cool for 30 minutes, then ladle out as much stock as possible into a sieve lined with cheesecloth or muslin. Remove the food solids and discard. Add 1 quart of cold water to the remaining stock, let stand for 10 minutes to allow the smaller particles to settle, and again ladle off as much stock as possible. Discard the dregs.

Taste for flavor. Reduce the stock if a stronger flavor is desired. Add salt to taste as a final step.

YIELD: about 12 quarts

NOTE: If beef and veal trimmings and chicken carcasses are not available, add more veal or beef bones, such as shin bones, preferably with meat on them.

It is not necessary to peel the vegetables, though they should be washed to remove any dirt. The skins of the onion will help to give the stock color.

Browning the bones before adding the liquid helps to ensure a richly colored stock.

Salt can be added to the stock; however, it is preferable to add it after the stock is made to prevent oversalting.

Chicken Stock

16 pounds chicken bones (see Note)
4 pounds veal bones (optional)
16 quarts water
8 carrots, sliced
8 onions, sliced
8 leeks, sliced

4 celery stalks, chopped
1 onion stuck with 4 cloves
4 bay leaves
8 sprigs parsley
8 sprigs fresh tarragon, or 1 tablespoon dried
salt and pepper, to taste

In a large kettle, combine the chicken bones, veal bones, and water. Bring slowly to a simmer, removing the scum as it appears. When it simmers, add the carrots, onions, leeks, celery, clove-studded onion, bay leaves, parsley, and tarragon. Return again to a boil, skimming the scum. Simmer for 1 to 2 hours.

Strain the stock, and chill. Remove and discard the fat. Correct seasoning with salt and pepper.

YIELD: 12 quarts

NOTE: To make a brown chicken stock, brown the chicken bones in a 475°F oven before proceeding.

If you can use the meat, whole chickens, fowls in particular, can be used in place of the bones. Remove the meat from the bones as soon as tender. Return bones to stock and simmer until done. Reserve the meat for other uses.

Fish Stock

12 pounds white fish bones	1 teaspoon dried thyme
8 stalks celery, chopped	8 bay leaves
8 cups chopped onions	¼ cup peppercorns
16 cloves garlic, crushed	8 cups dry white wine
½ bunch parsley, chopped	12 quarts cold water

In a stockpot, combine the fish bones, celery, onions, garlic, parsley, thyme, bay leaves, peppercorns, wine, and cold water. Bring to a boil, and simmer over low heat, uncovered, for 20 minutes, removing any scum that comes to the surface.

Strain through cheesecloth, discarding the bones and vegetables. YIELD: about 12 quarts

Vegetable Stock

½ cup olive oil	8 sprigs parsley
14 onions, minced	2 teaspoons thyme
12 parsnips, chopped	4 bay leaves
12 carrots, chopped	½ teaspoon cayenne pepper
12 white turnips, quartered	12 quarts water
8 stalks celery, chopped	salt and pepper, to taste

In a large kettle, heat the oil and sweat the onions until soft but not brown. Add the parsnips, carrots, turnips, celery, parsley, thyme, bay leaves, cayenne, and water. Bring to a boil and simmer for 1 hour.

Strain. Correct seasoning with salt and pepper.

YIELD: about 12 quarts

NOTE: Although this stock usually is used for vegetarian soups, it can be used in place of other stocks. The resulting flavor will be different, but not unsatisfactory.

❧ CONSOMMÉS ❧

Perfectly made consommé is one of the great treats of fine cuisine. It takes skill to create a full-flavored, crystal-clear, truly satisfying consommé.

Traditionally, consommé is served in handled bouillon cups so that diners can drink it if they choose. Cups also retain the heat better. Consommé should be almost at a boil when it is ladled into its cup—or soup plate, if necessary. It truly should be served too hot to eat so that it does not get cold in the time the diner is eating it.

Consommés are titled by the garnish served with them. Older cookbooks on *haute cuisine* list pages of consommés with truly elaborate garnishes which often require more work than they return in flavor. Today, with the interest in lighter foods, consommé should be at the top of the list of many menus.

On occasion, a consommé is thickened lightly with tapioca to give it more body. The current trend is to cook stocks with enough bones to give them a slightly sticky, gelatinous quality. Whether you garnish the consommé with a few poached vegetables, veal quenelles, or other garnish, remember that the consommé itself must be absolutely free of fat. If there is any sign of fat on the surface, touch the surface with paper toweling to take it up. If there is time, chill the consommé completely in order to remove any fat globules.

It is not uncommon to "finish" a consommé with a judicious application of a fortified wine such as port, Madeira, or sherry, or perhaps Cognac or rum. It must be added with care, however. Many a fine consommé has been ruined by a heavy hand with one of these. Add the wine in small amounts, tasting carefully after each addition until you just sense the flavor at the back of your throat. If you truly taste it, you have added too much. The point is to enhance the flavor of the consommé, not to overpower it.

Consommé

12 **quarts cold, strained beef stock**	8 **leeks, chopped**
6 **pounds ground, very lean beef**	8 **stalks celery, chopped**
4 **carrots, chopped**	12 **chicken backs, skinned (optional)**
	12 **egg whites and shells**

Remove and discard any fat from the stock. Put the stock into a pot with the ground beef, carrots, leeks, celery, chicken backs, and egg whites with their shells. Bring to a boil over medium heat, stirring constantly. As soon as the mixture comes to a boil, stop stirring. Let simmer for 1 hour, partially covered.

Line a colander with several thicknesses of very fine cheesecloth or muslin, and ladle in the stock and scum. Let the consommé drain.

The consommé can be reheated, garnished, and served immediately. Or it can be chilled until ready to serve.

YIELD: about 12 quarts

In the recipes that follow, the garnishes are chosen because they mate well with a particular flavor of consommé. But, in practice, you can usually substitute one garnish for another. An example is Consommé Aurore, which calls for julienne of chicken. This garnish would work equally well with a beef consommé. For a fish consommé, however, a better choice would be a julienne of fish.

You not only can, but should, make up your own garnishes. With imagination, you can create a garnish that will be a signature of your establishment. The recipes that follow are intended as much to stimulate your creativity as to grace your menus.

Consommé Balzac

6 quarts beef consommé
2 cups diced raw shrimp
2 cups cooked turnip balls
2 cups cooked petit pois

In a stockpot, bring the consommé to a boil, and add the garnishing ingredients. Turn off the heat, and let the retained heat finish the cooking.

For individual servings, a preferable method is as follows: Place the garnish in the consommé cup, and pour the boiling stock over it. The garnish cooks on its way to the table, and the shrimp will not be overcooked.

YIELD: 24 servings

Consommé Brancas

½ cup shredded lettuce
½ cup shredded sorrel
8 teaspoons butter (see Note)
4 cups stock, any flavor
½ cup broken vermicelli
½ cup julienned mushrooms
6 quarts consommé, any flavor
4 tablespoons minced fresh chervil, to garnish

In a skillet, sauté the lettuce and sorrel in 4 teaspoons of the butter until the liquid has evaporated.

Heat the stock and cook the vermicelli until *al dente*.

In a skillet, sauté the mushrooms in the remaining 4 teaspoons butter. When ready to serve, reheat the various garnish ingredients and add to the hot consommé. Top with a sprinkling of chervil.

YIELD: 24 servings

NOTE: Be stingy with the butter or it will form a film of oil on the surface of the consommé.

Consommé Brunoise

2 cups ¼-inch-diced carrots	2 cups ¼-inch-diced celery
2 cups ¼-inch-diced turnips	4 tablespoons butter
2 cups ¼-inch-diced leeks	6 quarts beef consommé

In a skillet, stew the carrots, turnips, leeks, celery, and butter until the vegetables are soft but not brown. Set aside.

When ready to serve, bring the consommé to a boil, add the garnish, and serve.

YIELD: 24 servings

Consommé au Cantaloupe (Cold Consommé with Cantaloupe)

6 quarts beef consommé	water, to cover
½ cup lemon juice	1 quart cantaloupe balls
salt and pepper, to taste	6 quarts cold beef consommé
8 carrots, julienne	mint sprigs, to garnish
8 stalks celery, julienne	

Combine the consommé with the lemon juice, and correct the seasoning with salt and pepper.

Blanch the carrots and celery in boiling salted water to cover until tender crisp. Drain.

Place some of the vegetable in individual consommé cups and top with the cantaloupe balls. Pour on the cold consommé.

Serve, or keep refrigerated until ready to serve. Serve garnished with a mint sprig.

YIELD: 24 servings

Consommé Carmen

4 tomatoes, peeled, seeded,
    and diced
4 red peppers, julienne
¼ cup cooked rice
6 quarts beef consommé

Prepare the garnish ingredients, and set aside. When ready to serve, heat the consommé and add the garnishes.
YIELD: 24 servings

NOTE: When chicken consommé is used in place of beef, the name is changed to Consommé à la Basquaise.

Consommé aux Cheveaux d'Ange (Consommé with Angel Hair Pasta)

6 quarts beef consommé
12 ounces angel hair pasta

Bring the consommé to a full rolling boil. Break the pasta into 2- to 3-inch lengths, and cook in the consommé until just done.
YIELD: 24 servings

NOTE: Good Italian durum wheat pasta has very little excess starch and will not cloud the consommé excessively. However, if you are using an unfamiliar brand or freshly made pasta, it is best to boil it in salted water until *al dente*, drain, rinse under cold water, and then add to the boiling consommé.

If desired, pass grated Parmesan cheese on the side.

Consommé Florence

6 quarts beef consommé
24 chipolata or tiny link sau-
    sages, cooked
¾ cup minced fresh chervil, to
    garnish

Heat the consommé. Place the sausages in a tureen or cup, and add the hot consommé. To serve, sprinkle with the chervil.
YIELD: 24 servings

NOTE: If small link sausages cannot be found, use kielbasa or other garlic sausage and cut into thin slices.

Consommé Madrilène

6 quarts beef or chicken stock   24 tomatoes, seeded and
3 pounds lean ground chuck   chopped
4 egg whites   ½ cup tomato puree
1 cup chopped carrots   cayenne pepper, to taste
3 leeks, chopped

In a stockpot, simmer the stock, ground beef, egg whites, carrots, leeks, and tomatoes for 1½ hours. Add the tomato puree.
   Line a fine sieve with a napkin wrung out in cold water, and strain the soup. Degrease the consommé, and season to taste with cayenne pepper.
   Chill until lightly set.
YIELD: 24 servings

Consommé Olga

2 cups julienne of celery root (see Note)	3 tablespoons butter
2 cups julienne of leek	1 cup julienne of cornichon
2 cups julienne of carrot	6 quarts beef consommé
	½ cup dry port, or to taste

In a saucepan, stew the celery root, leeks, and carrots with the butter, covered, until the vegetables are soft but not brown. Add to the consommé with the cornichon, and bring to a boil. Add just enough port to give a hint of flavor.

YIELD: 24 servings

NOTE: The vegetables must be in the thinnest possible strips. Cornichons are sour, pickled gherkins.

Consommé Saint-Quentin

8 hard-cooked eggs, sieved	2 cups flour, seasoned with salt and pepper
½ teaspoon grated nutmeg	
salt and pepper, to taste	butter, to sauté
2 teaspoons melted butter	6 quarts beef consommé
4 raw egg yolks	

In a bowl, mix the sieved egg, nutmeg, and salt and pepper to taste. Stir in the melted butter and enough of the egg yolk to make the mixture cohere.

Shape the mixture into ½-inch balls. Roll the balls in the seasoned flour, and sauté in butter until lightly browned, shaking the pan constantly. Drain on paper toweling.

When ready to serve, bring the consommé to a boil, and add the egg balls.

YIELD: 24 servings

NOTE: I believe that this consommé is named for the town of Saint-Quentin in the region of northern France called Picardy.

Consommé de Volaille
(Chicken Consommé)

12 quarts cold chicken stock
6 pounds chicken backs,
    skinned
4 carrots, chopped

8 leeks, chopped
8 stalks celery, chopped
12 egg whites and their shells

Remove any fat from the stock, and put the stock into a large pot. Add the chicken backs, carrots, leeks, celery, and egg whites with their shells, and bring slowly to a boil, stirring constantly. When the stock reaches the boil, stop stirring, lower heat, and simmer for 1 hour.

Line a colander with several thicknesses of fine cheesecloth or muslin, and set it over a large kettle. Carefully ladle the stock and the scum into the colander, and let the stock drain.

YIELD: about 12 quarts

Consommé Aurore

2 cups tomato puree
2 cups raw chicken, julienne
6 quarts chicken consommé

Stir the tomato puree and the chicken into the consommé, and heat until very hot. The chicken should just cook in the consommé, not overcook.

YIELD: 24 servings

NOTE: The tomato puree will cloud the consommé; do not expect it to be crystal clear. Do not attempt to add the tomato and then clarify the stock; after the clarifying, the tomato flavor would not be evident.

Consommé Borghese

3 chicken breasts, boned
3 cups chicken stock
120 asparagus tips
6 quarts chicken consommé

In a saucepan, poach the chicken breasts in the chicken stock until just barely cooked, about 8 minutes. Drain, and cut into fine julienne strips. Poach the asparagus tips in boiling salted water until tender crisp.

When ready to serve, heat the consommé, and add the chicken strips and asparagus tips.

YIELD: 24 servings

NOTE: Do not plan to poach the chicken in the consommé itself. The raw chicken will give off a scum that will cloud the consommé.

Essence of Celery

This sophisticated soup often is served with a cheese pastry such as cheese palmiers, sacristains, or pignatelles.

9 cups minced celery
1⅓ cups butter
9 cups chicken stock
salt and pepper, to taste

In a stockpot, sweat the celery and butter, covered, for 15 minutes. Do not let the celery brown. Add the chicken stock, and simmer for 30 minutes.

Strain the soup through several thicknesses of fine cheesecloth, and serve.

YIELD: 24 servings

Clam and Chicken Consommé

4 quarts chicken consommé
8 apples, quartered
   salt and pepper, to taste
6 cups clam broth
   generous pinch of cinnamon

3 to 6 cups whipped cream,
   unsweetened, to
   garnish
   grated nutmeg, to
   garnish

In a pot, simmer the consommé, apples, and salt and pepper to taste for 1 hour. Puree in a blender, processor, or food mill. Strain and stir in the clam broth, reheat, and season to taste with cinnamon.

Garnish each serving with a generous dollop of whipped cream sprinkled with nutmeg.

YIELD: 24 servings

Consommé Diablotins
(Consommé with Cheese Toast)

24 ¼-inch-thick slices French
   bread
 8 teaspoons butter
 2 cups grated Gruyère cheese
 6 cups hot chicken consommé

Preheat the broiler. Spread the bread with butter, and sprinkle with the cheese. Arrange on a baking sheet, and broil until the cheese is bubbly and golden.

When ready to serve, pour the hot consommé into the bowl, and float a cheese toast on top.

YIELD: 24 servings

Consommé Eugénie

4 quarts chicken consommé
1 cup thinly sliced carrots
1 cup thinly sliced celery
1 cup thinly sliced mushrooms
2 cups peeled, seeded, and
    finely diced tomatoes

4 teaspoons minced fresh
    parsley
4 teaspoons minced fresh
    chervil

In a stockpot, simmer the consommé, carrots, and celery for 10 minutes or until the vegetables are tender crisp. Add the mushrooms and tomatoes, and simmer 1 minute. Sprinkle with the parsley and chervil, and serve.

YIELD: 24 servings

Consommé Mimosa

4 hard-cooked eggs
½ cup minced parsley
6 quarts chicken consommé

Separate the whites from the yolks of the eggs and put them through a sieve separately, to keep the colors distinct.

In a bowl, mix the sieved egg white, egg yolk, and minced parsley together.

When ready to serve, ladle the hot soup into the bowls, and sprinkle with a teaspoon of the garnish.

YIELD: 24 servings

NOTE: If you sieve the egg yolk and white separately, you will have two distinct colors. If you sieve the whole egg, it will come out pale yellow.

Consommé aux Primeurs
(Early Vegetable Consommé)

6 quarts chicken consommé	1 cup thinly sliced scallions
2 cups julienne of carrots	2 tablespoons minced parsley
2 cups green peas	salt and pepper, to taste
2 cups shredded spinach leaves	½ cup minced fresh summer savory (optional)

In a stockpot, bring the consommé to a boil, and simmer the carrots and peas for 4 minutes. Add the spinach, scallions, and parsley, and simmer 2 minutes. Correct the seasoning with salt, pepper, and savory.

YIELD: 24 servings

NOTE: If fresh savory is not available, omit it.

Consommé Printanier
(Spring Vegetable Consommé)

6 quarts chicken consommé	½ cup asparagus tips
2 cups tiny carrot sticks (see Note)	1 quart shredded sorrel leaves
2 cups tiny turnip sticks	1 quart shredded Boston lettuce leaves
½ cup diced string beans	
½ cup tiny peas	

Bring the consommé to a boil, add the carrots and turnips, and simmer 2 minutes. Add the beans and peas, and simmer 1 minute. Add the asparagus, sorrel, and lettuce, and simmer 2 minutes.

Serve immediately.

YIELD: 24 servings

NOTE: The carrots and turnips should be cut ⅛ inch thick and 1 inch long.

If the consommé cannot be served immediately, cook the various ingredients separately and set aside. Add a small portion of each to each bowl as it is served.

Consommé aux Profiteroles

144 unfilled, unsweetened,
½-inch cream puffs
6 cups chicken consommé

Float the puffs in the hot soup just before serving.
YIELD: 24 servings

NOTE: Although this recipe calls for unfilled puffs, you can fill them with a chicken forcemeat or a cheese paste. Pureed chicken liver makes a delicious filling.

Consommé Rejane

6 quarts chicken consommé
2 cups julienne of leeks (see
  Note)
1 cup julienne of potatoes
1 quart julienne of chicken

Bring the consommé to a simmer and add the leeks and potatoes. Simmer 4 minutes, or until just barely tender, and add the chicken. Cook for about 1 minute or until the chicken is just cooked.
YIELD: 24 servings

NOTE: All of the ingredients should be cut into the finest possible shreds. If necessary, the leek and potato can be cooked separately and allowed to cool. When ready to serve, add them to the hot consommé with the uncooked chicken. If the consommé is hot enough it will cook the chicken while the soup is being served.

❧ CREAM SOUPS ❧

Velvety smooth cream soups, unctuous and delicate with a satisfying richness, are always in demand. They are elegant enough for the most elite dinner party. Or they can serve as a replete luncheon or supper accompanied with a beautiful salad or some tea sandwiches.

The bases for many cream soups can be made ahead in quantity and you can flavor them according to the day's menu or the availability of ingredients. Even with today's interest in lighter cuisine, people still love cream soups. They are nourishing and—when made correctly—they are light on the tongue.

Although most of the recipes in this section do not specify it, many cream soups will benefit from the careful addition of a fortified wine such as sherry, port, or Madeira. Take care that the wine is added in small quantities and that you do not overpower the soup with it. You should sense the wine at the back of the throat, rather than taste it on the tongue. It goes without saying that the wine should be of good quality. If you would not drink it, then do not use it in cooking.

There are four principal types of cream soups: shellfish purees, or bisques; vegetable purees; veloutés; and creams.

BISQUES AND PUREES

Bisques are made from cooking minced vegetables with some type of shellfish (and their shells) and rice to thicken the soup. The bisque is strained and then enriched with cream. On occasion the bisque is thickened with fish velouté or sautéed breadcrumbs rather than rice. The shells alone have enough flavor to make a bisque. Thus it is possible to make a superb soup with shrimp shells or lobster shells that would usually be discarded. Bisques do not fit solely into this rather tight definition. It would be impossible to make a bisque out of clam or oyster shells, so those bisques are made differently, as you will see in the recipes.

Vegetable purees are similar to bisques except that the soup usually has a vegetable base and the thickening comes from the principal vegetable itself or from the addition of a starchy food such as potatoes or beans.

VELOUTÉS

Veloutés are based on a cream sauce flavored with a chicken or fish stock. This is combined with a vegetable puree to make the soup. This method allows you to prepare almost any flavored vegetable cream soup. The veloutés are finished with an egg yolk-and-cream liaison to bind and enrich the soup.

CREAMS

These soups combine a basic element—usually a vegetable, meat, or fish puree—with a full-flavored stock that is thickened with egg yolk and cream. They can also be made by reducing the stock and cream to a delicate coating consistency, a method currently very popular in many restaurants. Some cooks object to the latter method, however, because of the amount of fat that results from the reduction of the cream. A cream soup should be impressive for its delicate smoothness—a quality that is deceptive, however, since the cream soups are not light in calories. None of these soups would qualify as spa cuisine.

Which is the best method to use? The choice is yours. You may feel that for the rest of the menu the subtle nuances of a cream suit better than the fuller quality of a velouté or bisque, or you may just need to use up cream. One point should be made clear. There is no best type, only different types. Each of the preparations is superb in its own way.

No matter which method you follow, you ought to garnish each serving with some of the principal ingredient. A slice of lobster for

Lobster Bisque, perfectly cooked asparagus tips for Cream of Asparagus Soup, or poached mussels for Billi Bi.

TEMPERATURE

Just as consommés have a correct temperature at which to be served (extremely hot), so do cream soups. They should be served hot but not boiling. If a soup with an egg yolk-cream liaison is boiled, it will curdle. Also, because the cream soups are thicker and have a more complete coating consistency, they can easily burn guests' mouths. I recommend that the soups be served at 140°F to 150°F.

Clam Bisque

½ teaspoon cayenne pepper	1 cup butter
½ teaspoon dry mustard	1 cup flour
½ teaspoon celery seed	1 cup dry white wine
½ teaspoon salt	½ cup minced fresh basil, or
½ teaspoon pepper	to taste
130 cherrystone clams	salt and pepper, to taste
4 quarts milk, scalded	minced parsley, to garnish

In a small bowl, mix the cayenne pepper, dry mustard, celery seed, salt, and pepper. Set aside.

In a large kettle, steam the clams in ½ inch of water until the shells open. Discard any unopened clams. Open the clams over the pot, and let the clam liquor fall back into it. Place the clam meat in a bowl, and discard the shells. Mince the clams.

Add the milk to the clam liquor, and reheat but do not boil.

In another stockpot, melt the butter, add the flour, and cook over low heat, stirring, to make a roux. Add the hot milk and the wine, stirring, and bring to a boil, stirring constantly. Add the minced clams, basil, and salt and pepper to taste.

Serve garnished with the parsley.

YIELD: 24 servings

NOTE: To make a *nouvelle* version of this soup, substitute 8 quarts of heavy cream reduced to 4 quarts in place of the milk, butter, and flour.

The basil should flavor the soup delicately and not overpower the clam flavor.

Clam and Mushroom Bisque

6 pounds mushrooms, sliced	3 cups heavy cream
¾ pound butter	dry sherry to taste
¼ cup flour	salt and pepper, to taste
4 quarts clam broth	

Sweat the mushrooms in the butter until very tender. Add the flour, and cook, stirring, for 10 minutes over medium heat. Do not let the flour brown.

Add the broth, and simmer for 10 minutes, stirring constantly. Puree the soup, and return to a clean stockpot.

Stir in the cream and reheat. Add just enough sherry to enhance it without overwhelming it. Correct the seasoning with salt and pepper.

YIELD: 24 servings

Bisque d'Homard
(Lobster Bisque)

12 lobster carcasses	4 dried hot red peppers
½ cup olive oil	1⅓ cups flour
½ cup butter	3 cups Cognac
1 quart chopped onion	2 quarts white wine
1 cup thinly sliced shallots	3 quarts chopped tomatoes
3 cups chopped carrots	1 gallon water
1 quart chopped celery	½ bunch parsley
4 bay leaves	2 cups rice
4 teaspoons minced garlic	6 cups heavy cream
2 teaspoons dried thyme	4 lobster tails, cooked and
¼ cup peppercorns	thinly sliced, to garnish

Chop the carcasses into 2- to 3-inch pieces, and set aside.

In a skillet, heat the oil and butter, and sweat the onions, shallots, carrots, celery, bay leaves, garlic, thyme, and peppercorns.

Add the lobster carcasses and red peppers. Sprinkle with the flour, and stir to distribute evenly. Add 2 cups of the Cognac, the wine, tomatoes, water, and parsley, and bring to a boil. Add the rice, and simmer 20 minutes, covered. Discard the larger, harder pieces of shell, and force the mixture through a food mill on the finest blade, pressing to extract as much liquid as possible. Discard the solids.

For a smoother finish, strain the soup through a fine sieve after it has been put through the food mill, or force it through several thicknesses of cheesecloth.

Reheat the bisque, stir in the cream, and correct the seasoning with salt and pepper. Add the remaining Cognac and bring almost to a boil.

Serve garnished with lobster slices.

YIELD: 24 servings

Bisque de Crabe
(Crab Bisque)

Substitute 3 pounds of cleaned, chopped crab and its shell for the lobster. Garnish with pieces of lump crabmeat.

Bisque de Crevettes I
(Shrimp Bisque I)

Substitute 2 pounds of shrimp for the lobster carcasses, or use the shells from 4 pounds of shrimp. Garnish the soup with poached shrimp.

Oyster and Spinach Bisque

1 quart oysters	1½ pounds spinach, stripped
3 cups minced onions	6 cups milk
¾ cup minced shallots	3 cups heavy cream
¾ cup butter	salt and pepper, to taste
1¼ cups flour	pinch of grated nutmeg
3 cups dry white wine	pinch of cayenne pepper

Drain the oysters, reserving both the meat and the liquor.

In a stockpot, sweat the onions and shallots in the butter, stir in the flour, and cook, stirring, until foamy. Add the wine and oyster liquor, stirring rapidly. Simmer 10 minutes.

Add the spinach, and cook 1 minute. Add the oysters and milk, and bring just to a boil.

Puree the soup. Return the soup to the pot, and add the cream, salt and pepper to taste, nutmeg, and cayenne.

Serve hot.

YIELD: 24 servings

NOTE: If desired, serve a poached oyster in each cup. Or whip heavy cream, and put a dollop of cream on top crowned with a poached oyster.

Bisque de Crevettes II
(Shrimp Bisque II)

2 cups minced carrots	4 pounds shrimp
2 cups minced onions	6 quarts fish velouté (see recipe, page 43)
½ bunch parsley	ipe, page 43)
2 bay leaves	milk, if required
1 tablespoon thyme	1 cup cream
½ cup butter	½ cup butter
1 quart dry white wine	½ cup Cognac or Madeira

In a saucepan, sweat the carrots, onions, parsley, bay leaves, and thyme in the butter until tender.

Add the wine and shrimp, and poach the shrimp until they turn pink. Remove the shrimp, and allow to cool. Peel and devein the shrimp, adding the shells to the liquid.

Puree the meat of 2 pounds of shrimp, and add to the soup with the velouté base. Simmer 20 minutes.

Strain through a very fine sieve. If the soup is too thick, add enough milk to thin to the desired consistency. Strain again through several thicknesses of cheesecloth.

Just before serving, reheat the soup, and add the cream, butter, and Cognac or Madeira.

Garnish each serving with reserved shrimp.

YIELD: 24 to 30 servings

Crème d'Artichauts
(Cream of Artichoke Soup)

32 artichokes	4 quarts heavy cream
4 lemons, sliced	½ cup butter
juice of 4 lemons	½ cup flour
1½ cups olive oil	salt and pepper, to taste
¼ cup salt	

Trim the artichokes, and remove any dried leaves.

In a large casserole, combine the artichokes, lemons, lemon juice, olive oil, and ¼ cup salt. Simmer 30 to 45 minutes or until the artichokes are tender.

Drain, discarding the cooking liquid. Rinse the artichokes. When they are cool enough to handle, remove the leaves and discard the choke.

Scrape the meat from each leaf and puree together with the hearts.

Bring the cream to a boil, stir in the puree, and simmer 5 minutes. Make a *beurre manié* from the butter and flour, and add it in small bits to the simmering soup until the soup is thickened. It may not be necessary to use all the *beurre manié*. Correct the seasoning with salt and pepper.

YIELD: 24 servings

Potage Crème d'Artichauts
(Cream of Artichoke Soup)

4 cups minced onions	salt and pepper, to taste
4 cups minced leeks	6 quarts chicken stock
1⅓ cups minced celery	1 quart milk
2 cups butter	1 quart light cream
36 artichoke bottoms, diced	minced parsley, to garnish

In a stockpot, sweat the onions, leeks, and celery in 1½ cups butter, covered, for 20 minutes or until the vegetables are very tender but not colored.

Add the diced artichoke bottoms, and simmer 5 minutes. Season to taste with salt and pepper, and add the chicken stock. Simmer for 30 minutes. Puree through a food mill, and return to a clean stockpot. Add the milk and cream, and bring to a simmer. Swirl in the remaining ½ cup butter, and serve garnished with the parsley.
YIELD: 24 servings

Crème Vichy aux Pois
(Cream of Carrot Soup with Peas)

1 cup butter	2 tablespoons minced chervil
4 pounds carrots, shredded	3 teaspoons minced marjoram
4 bunches scallions, minced	2 teaspoons minced thyme
3 cups minced shallots	8 quarts chicken stock
4 potatoes, minced	1 quart heavy cream
4 garlic cloves, minced	1 quart tiny peas, cooked
2 tablespoons minced tarragon	salt and pepper, to taste

In a pot, sweat the carrots, scallions, shallots, potatoes, garlic, tarragon, chervil, marjoram, and thyme in the butter until soft.

Add the stock and simmer, uncovered, until the potatoes are tender.

Puree the soup. Return to the pot and bring to a simmer. Add the cream and peas and correct the seasoning with salt and pepper.
YIELD: 24 servings

NOTE: The herb measurements are for fresh herbs. If you must use dried herbs, reduce the quantities by one-third.

Crème d'Aubergines
(Cream of Eggplant Soup)

6 cups diced onions	1 teaspoon thyme
6 cups diced celery	3 tablespoons minced fresh
4 large eggplants, peeled and	basil
diced	¾ cup butter
6 cups diced potatoes	4 quarts chicken stock
2 teaspoons curry powder	1 quart heavy cream

In a stockpot, sweat the onions, celery, eggplants, potatoes, curry powder, thyme, and basil in the butter.

Stir in the stock, and cook, uncovered, for 45 minutes or until all the ingredients are very soft.

Puree the soup, and stir in the cream.

YIELD: 24 servings

NOTE: If desired, sauté a peeled, diced eggplant in butter until golden and use to garnish the soup.

Cream of Leek and Watercress Soup

6 cups minced leeks	8 bunches watercress, chopped
4 cups minced onion	3 quarts chicken stock
6 garlic cloves, minced	1 quart milk
salt and pepper, to taste	1 quart heavy cream
1 cup butter	watercress sprigs, to garnish
8 potatoes, thinly sliced	

In a stockpot, sweat the leeks, onions, and garlic, together with the salt and pepper, in the butter for 20 minutes or until the vegetables are very soft. Add the potatoes, chopped watercress, and stock, and simmer 25 minutes.

Puree the mixture, and return to a clean stockpot. Add the milk and cream, and bring to a simmer. Correct the seasoning with salt and pepper.

Serve garnished with sprigs of watercress.
YIELD: 24 servings

Onion Puree

6 quarts thinly sliced onions	6 bay leaves
¾ pound butter	¾ cup instant Cream of Rice
salt, to taste	1½ quarts milk
3 quarts chicken stock	nutmeg, to taste
1½ teaspoons thyme	white pepper, to taste

In a stockpot, sweat the onions, butter, and salt to taste, covered, for about 15 minutes or until the onions are very soft but not browned.

Add the stock, thyme, and bay leaves, and bring to a boil. Sprinkle on the Cream of Rice, and simmer, covered, for 20 minutes. Remove and discard the bay leaves, and stir in the milk, nutmeg, and white pepper.

Puree the soup, and strain through a fine sieve.
YIELD: 24 servings

Cream of Parsnip Soup

4 onions, chopped	4 pounds parsnips, chopped
4 leeks, chopped	4 potatoes, chopped
4 chili peppers, chopped	5½ quarts hot water
2 teaspoons sugar	1½ quarts chicken stock
2 teaspoons minced gingerroot	1½ cups yogurt
	salt and pepper, to taste
½ teaspoon turmeric	¼ tablespoon minced pista-
⅛ teaspoon grated nutmeg	chio nuts, to garnish
½ cup butter	

In a stockpot, sweat the onions, leeks, chili peppers, sugar, gingerroot, turmeric, and nutmeg in the butter until soft but not brown. Add the parsnips and potatoes, and cook 5 minutes.

Add the water and stock, and simmer until the parsnips and potatoes are tender, about 20 minutes. Allow to cool slightly.

Puree the soup, then press through a fine sieve. Add the yogurt, correct the seasoning with salt and pepper, and reheat gently.

Sprinkle each serving with nuts.

YIELD: 24 servings

Curried Pea and Avocado Soup

1 cup minced onions	salt and pepper, to taste
1½ tablespoons curry powder	2 quarts chicken stock
¾ cup butter	3 avocados, pureed
2 quarts shelled green peas	1 quart light cream
1 tablespoon dried chervil	3 avocados, sliced

In a stockpot, sauté the onion and curry powder in the butter until the onion is soft but not brown. Add the peas, chervil, salt and pepper to taste, and chicken stock, and simmer, covered, for 20 minutes or until the peas are very tender. Puree the soup, and add the avocado puree.

Return the soup to the stockpot, add the cream, and correct the seasoning with salt and pepper. Reheat.

Serve with a slice of avocado.

YIELD: 24 servings

Puree de Saint-Germain
(Cream of Pea Soup)

3 quarts chicken stock	½ cup minced fresh mint
6 pound peas, shelled	4 teaspoons sugar
4 onions, minced	½ pound butter
4 carrots, minced	2 cups heavy cream
8 lettuce leaves, shredded	

In a stockpot, simmer the stock, peas, onions, carrots, lettuce, mint, and sugar until the vegetables are tender.

Puree the soup, and stir in the butter and cream. Reheat slowly.

For a smoother soup, strain through a fine sieve.

YIELD: 24 servings

NOTE: Can be served hot or cold. The flavor is enhanced by a judicious addition of dry sherry.

Cream of Fresh Green Pea Soup with Chicken

2 6-pound chickens	water, to cover
salt and pepper, to taste	1½ tablespoons sugar
½ cup melted butter	8 quarts milk
12 pounds fresh peas, shelled	salt and pepper, to taste
50 pea pods	2 cups toasted fresh bread-
16 small white onions,	crumbs, to garnish
chopped	minced fresh chervil, to
8 heads Boston lettuce	garnish

Sprinkle the chickens with salt and pepper, and brush with the melted butter. Roast at 400°F, turning often until cooked, about 1½ hours. Set aside.

In a stockpot, place the peas, pea pods, onions, lettuce, and sugar. Cover with salted water, and simmer until the vegetables are very tender, about 20 minutes. Drain, reserving 2 cups of the liquid, and discard the pea pods.

Puree the peas, lettuce, and onions. Stir 1 cup of the reserved liquid into the puree. In a clean stockpot, mix the pea puree with enough milk to make a creamy soup. If needed, add the remaining cup of reserved liquid. Reheat. Remove the meat from the chickens, and cut into slivers. Add to the soup.

Serve the soup sprinkled with breadcrumbs and chervil.

YIELD: 24 servings

Puree de Germiny
(Cream of Potato and Sorrel Soup)

1 quart chopped onions	4 pounds sorrel leaves,
¼ cup butter	shredded
6 pounds potatoes, peeled	1 quart heavy cream
and diced	salt and pepper, to taste
5 quarts chicken stock	

In a stockpot, sweat the onions in the butter. Add the potatoes and stock, and stir in half the sorrel. Cook for 20 minutes and puree.

Reheat the soup, and add the cream and salt and pepper to taste, and bring almost to a boil. Stir in the remaining sorrel.

Serve hot or cold.

YIELD: 24 servings

Potage de Potiron
(Puree of Pumpkin Soup)

6 pounds pumpkin, cut up	1 cup chopped spinach
2 cups sliced potatoes	1 cup chopped leeks
4 quarts water	1 cup cooked rice
4 quarts heavy cream	1 cup cooked peas
1¼ pounds butter	¼ cup minced parsley
1 cup chopped sorrel	salt and pepper, to taste

In a stockpot, simmer the pumpkin and potatoes in the water until tender.

Puree the vegetables, and stir in the cream and 1 pound of the butter.

In the remaining ¼ pound of butter sweat the sorrel, spinach, and leeks until the butter is absorbed. Add to the soup with the rice, peas, parsley, and salt and pepper to taste.

Serve hot.

YIELD: 24 servings

Cream of Ramp Soup

Ramp, a relative of the garlic family, is found principally in and around West Virginia, where it has a short season in the early spring. The flavor is considered somewhat pervasive but truly special. If you can obtain ramps, try this soup for a spectacular soup course.

2½ pounds ramps, minced	4 quarts chicken stock
½ pound butter	5 cups heavy cream
3¾ pounds boiling potatoes	salt, to taste

Set aside ½ cup of minced ramps for a garnish.

In a stockpot, sweat the remaining ramps in the butter until soft. Add the potatoes and the chicken stock, and simmer 30 minutes.

Puree the soup, stir in the cream, and reheat. Correct the seasoning with salt. Force the soup through a fine sieve.

Serve garnished with the reserved raw ramps.

YIELD: 24 servings

Velouté Base for Fish Soups

3 cups butter
3 cups flour
8 quarts fish stock

In a stockpot, melt the butter and gradually stir in the flour. Cook the roux until it gets foamy and starts to turn golden. Add the stock, and cook, stirring, until the mixture is smooth and thick.

Simmer 20 minutes, skimming and stirring as needed. Strain through a fine sieve.

YIELD: 9 quarts fish velouté

Potage Jacqueline

7 quarts fish velouté	2 cups cooked peas, to garnish
8 egg yolks	1 cup cooked rice, to garnish
2 cups heavy cream	
2 cups cooked diced carrots, to garnish	

In a stockpot, heat the velouté just to the boiling point. Mix the egg yolks and cream together, and add to the soup, stirring. Heat to just below the boiling point.

Serve each portion garnished with carrots, peas, and rice.

YIELD: 24 servings

Fonds de Crème de Volaille or Velouté de Volaille (Cream of Chicken Base)

1 cup butter	4 veal knuckles (optional)
2 cups Cream of Rice	any chicken bones (optional)
2 gallons chicken stock	8 stalks celery, chopped
16 leeks, chopped	salt, to taste

In a stockpot, melt the butter, stir in the Cream of Rice, and cook, stirring, until the cereal starts to turn golden.

Add the chicken stock, and cook, stirring, until the mixture just comes to a boil. Add the leeks, veal or chicken bones, and celery, and cook, stirring occasionally, for 1½ to 2 hours.

Strain through a food mill.
YIELD: 6 quarts of chicken velouté base

NOTE: Use this base to make almost any cream of vegetable soup. The recipes below are suggestions. Use your imagination. The Cream of Rice gives the soup a texture different from one made with flour. Flour can be used, as can Cream of Wheat, however. If you use one of the cereals, take care to stir often as the mixture comes to a boil and thickens, otherwise the cereal is likely to settle and burn on the bottom of the pot.

To Use the Base

Flavor the base by cooking about 2 quarts of the vegetables of your choice in the strained base until very tender. Strain through a food mill and finish with a liaison of 8 egg yolks and 1 to 2 quarts of heavy cream. Beat the eggs with 1 quart of the cream and add to the hot soup. Heat until almost boiling, stirring often. Strain again. If the soup is too thick, add the additional quart of cream; if it is still too thick, thin it with stock or milk.

Vegetables for the Base

Some vegetables can be added raw, such as beans, peas, or carrots. Other vegetables—especially those with a stronger flavor such as broccoli, cauliflower, or celery—should be blanched for about 5 minutes. Sauté mushrooms in butter to bring out their flavor before adding to the base. Roasting peppers before adding to the base brings out their flavor.

It is wise to cook some of the vegetables in stock to use as a garnish for the soup, such as broccoli florets or asparagus tips. The soups can often be enhanced with a careful addition of a fortified wine such as Madeira or sherry.

Velouté d'Asperges
(Cream of Asparagus Soup)

4 pounds asparagus stems, chopped (see Note)	8 egg yolks
6 quarts cream of chicken base (see recipe, page 44)	1 to 2 quarts heavy cream
	salt and pepper, to taste
	Madeira, to taste

Blanch the asparagus in boiling, salted water for 5 minutes. Set any tips aside as garnish.

Simmer the remainder of the asparagus in the chicken base until tender. Strain through a food mill, and strain again through a sieve. Make the liaison with the egg yolks and 1 quart of heavy cream. Add the remaining cream if needed. Correct the seasoning with salt, pepper, and Madeira. Strain again.

YIELD: 24 servings

NOTE: The soup can be made from vegetable parts that are usually discarded, in this case, asparagus stems.

Crème d'Avocats
(Cream of Avocado Soup)

6 quarts cream of chicken soup base (see recipe, page 44)	6 egg yolks
	salt and pepper, to taste
6 avocados, peeled	sautéed croutons, to accompany

Heat the soup. Puree the avocado in a processor. Add the egg yolks to the avocado, and process again. When the avocado mixture is very smooth, ladle 3 cups of the hot soup, 1 cup at a time, into the container while continuing to process. Return the mixture to the hot soup, blend well, and season to taste with salt and pepper. Be careful not to boil the soup. Pass the croutons, separately.

YIELD: 24 servings

Crème du Barry
_____(Cream of Cauliflower Soup)_____

4 cauliflower heads, chopped	8 egg yolks
6 quarts cream of chicken base (see recipe, page 44)	1 to 2 quarts heavy cream salt and pepper, to taste

Blanch the cauliflower in boiling, salted water for 5 minutes. Drain.

Set aside 1 cup of tiny florets to garnish the soup. Simmer the remaining cauliflower in the chicken base until very tender. Force through a food mill.

Mix the egg yolks and 1 quart of heavy cream, and add to the soup. Add remaining cream if needed to thin. Correct the seasoning with salt and pepper.

Serve, garnished with florets.

YIELD: 24 servings

Velouté de Fenouil
_____(Cream of Fennel)_____

24 fennel bulbs, thinly sliced	8 egg yolks
½ pound butter	1 to 2 quarts heavy cream
6 quarts cream of chicken base (see recipe, page 44)	salt and pepper, to taste minced chives, to garnish

Braise the fennel in the butter over low heat, covered, until very soft and lightly browned.

Puree. Add to the chicken base, and simmer 30 minutes.

Strain, and make the liaison with the egg yolks and 1 quart of the heavy cream. Add the remaining cream if needed to thin. Correct the seasoning with salt and pepper, and garnish with the chives.

YIELD: 24 servings

Crème Favorite
(Cream of Green Bean Soup)

2 quarts green beans, chopped
6 quarts cream of chicken
    base (see recipe, page 44)
8 egg yolks

1 to 2 quarts heavy cream
    salt and pepper, to taste
    green beans, to garnish

In a stockpot, simmer the green beans in the base until very tender. Force through a food mill, and return to the pot.

Make the liaison with the egg yolks and 1 quart of the heavy cream. Add additional cream, if needed, to thin. Strain. Correct the seasoning with salt and pepper.

Garnish the soup with some blanched, diced green beans.

YIELD: 24 servings

Crème Laitue
(Cream of Lettuce)

16 heads Boston lettuce,
    shredded
6 quarts cream of chicken
    base (see recipe, page 44)
    salt and pepper, to taste

8 egg yolks
1 to 2 quarts heavy cream
    lemon juice, to taste
1 cup fried croutons, to
    accompany

Plunge 1 quart of the greenest leaves from the shredded lettuce into boiling, salted water. Bring to a boil, drain, rinse with cold water, and drain again. Dry on toweling, and set aside to use as a garnish.

Cook the remaining lettuce in the soup base for 1 hour. Strain through a food mill. Season to taste with salt and pepper.

Make the liaison with the egg yolks and 1 quart of the heavy cream. If needed, add more cream. Correct the seasoning with lemon juice, salt, and pepper.

Serve the soup garnished with the reserved lettuce leaves, and pass the croutons separately.

YIELD: 24 servings

Crème de Morilles
(Cream of Morels)

12 ounces dried morels
2 cups dry white wine
2 cups lukewarm water
1½ cups minced shallots
2 cups butter

2 cups flour
  salt and pepper, to taste
4 quarts chicken stock
8 egg yolks
1 quart heavy cream

Soak the morels in the wine and water for 2 hours. Drain. Strain the liquid through a coffee filter, and reserve. Remove and discard the stems of the morels. Halve the morels lengthwise, and rinse to remove any grit. Drain again, and cut into ¼-inch dice.

In a large saucepan, sweat the morels and shallots in the butter until softened. Add the flour, and cook, stirring, 3 minutes. Raise the heat, and add the salt and pepper to taste and the stock together with the reserved morel liquid. Cook, stirring, until thickened and smooth. Simmer, uncovered, for 30 minutes, stirring occasionally. Make the liaison with the egg yolks and the cream, and add to the soup.

YIELD: 24 servings

Crème Forestière
(Cream of Mushroom Soup)

4 onions, minced
2 pounds mushrooms,
  minced
¼ cup butter
6 quarts cream of chicken
  base (see recipe, page 44)

8 egg yolks
1 to 2 quarts heavy cream
  salt and pepper, to taste
  port, to taste
3 cups sliced mushrooms,
  sautéed in butter, to
  garnish

In a stockpot, sauté the onions and mushrooms in the butter until the liquid has evaporated. Add the chicken base, and simmer 1 hour.

Force the soup through a food mill. Make the liaison with the egg yolks and 1 quart of heavy cream. Add more cream if needed to thin.

Strain. Correct the seasoning with salt, pepper, and port.

Serve garnished with the sautéed mushroom slices.

YIELD: 24 servings

Crème Calcutta

4 pounds onions, sliced	1 quart milk
½ cup butter	3 cups cooked rice
8 teaspoons curry powder	2 to 4 cups heavy cream
4 quarts cream of chicken base (see recipe, page 44)	4 red Delicious apples, finely diced, to garnish

Blanch the onions in boiling, salted water for 5 minutes. Drain.

In a stockpot, sweat the onions in the butter until very soft but not brown. Stir in the curry powder, and cook, stirring, for 5 minutes. Add the chicken base, and simmer for 5 minutes. Stir in the milk and rice, and stir in enough cream to achieve the desired consistency.

Serve hot, garnished with the diced apples.

YIELD: 24 servings

NOTE: To keep apples for garnish from turning brown, put in acidulated water until ready to use.

Crème Saint-Germain
_____(Cream of Pea Soup)_____

4 pounds peas, shelled
6 quarts cream of chicken
    base (see recipe, page 44)
8 egg yolks

1 to 2 quarts heavy cream
    salt and pepper, to taste
    sherry, to taste

In a stockpot, simmer the peas in the chicken base until tender. Force through a food mill.

Make the liaison with the egg yolks and 1 quart of the heavy cream, and stir into the soup. Add more cream, if needed, to thin. Correct the seasoning with salt, pepper, and sherry. Strain.
YIELD: 24 servings

Potage Vert Pré
_____(Green Meadow Soup)_____

2 cups minced scallions
¾ cup butter
¾ cup flour
4 quarts peas, shelled
4 heads Boston lettuce,
    shredded
1 quart spinach leaves,
    shredded

¼ cup sugar
6 quarts chicken stock
    salt, to taste
1 quart heavy cream
12 egg yolks
    pepper, to taste
1 quart cooked peas

In a stockpot, sauté the scallions in the butter until tender. Stir in the flour, and cook, stirring, for 2 minutes. Add the fresh peas, lettuce, spinach, sugar, stock, and salt to taste. Simmer, covered, for 45 minutes.

Puree the soup. Make a liaison with the cream and egg yolks, add to soup, and heat the soup almost to the boiling point. Correct the seasoning with salt and pepper. Stir in the cooked peas.
YIELD: 24 servings

Crème de Champignons
(Mushroom Cream Soup)

½ cup minced onions
2 pounds minced mushrooms
4 teaspoons lemon juice
½ cup butter
4 quarts chicken stock
½ cup minced parsley

1 quart heavy cream
8 egg yolks
  salt and pepper, to taste
2 cups sliced raw mush-
  rooms, to garnish

In a stockpot, stew the onions, mushrooms, and lemon juice in the butter until the onions and mushrooms are soft but not brown. Add the stock and parsley, and simmer 20 minutes.

Puree the soup. Make the liaison with the cream and egg yolks, and add to the soup. Correct the seasoning with salt and pepper, and serve garnished with slices of raw mushrooms.
YIELD: 20 servings

NOTE: The soup may be served hot or cold.

Potage Germiny
(Cream of Sorrel Soup)

4 pounds sorrel leaves,
  shredded
1 cup butter
2 cups minced onions
3 quarts chicken stock

8 egg yolks
1 quart heavy cream
  Tabasco, to taste
  salt and pepper, to taste

In a stockpot, sauté the onion in the butter until soft but not brown. Stir in the sorrel, and cook until wilted. Add the stock, and simmer 10 minutes.

Make the liaison with the egg yolks and cream, and add to the soup. Correct the seasoning with Tabasco, salt, and pepper.
YIELD: 24 servings

_____Cream of Squash Soup_____

6 pounds Hubbard squash,
   peeled and cubed
1 quart milk
1 quart heavy cream
1 quart chicken stock
1 cup honey
¼ cup Cognac

2 teaspoons grated orange
   rind
1 teaspoon ground ginger
1 teaspoon ground mace
1 teaspoon ground nutmeg
   salt and pepper, to taste

Cook the squash in boiling salted water until tender. Drain and puree.

Stir the milk into the puree with the cream, stock, honey, cognac, orange rind, ginger, nutmeg, mace, and salt to taste. Reheat, and correct the seasoning with salt and pepper.

Serve hot or cold.

YIELD: 24 servings

_____Hot or Cold Cream of Tomato Soup_____

4 onions, minced
¼ cup butter
24 tomatoes, peeled, seeded,
   and chopped
4 cups chicken stock
2 teaspoons tomato paste
1½ teaspoons sugar
2 teaspoons minced thyme
   salt, to taste

3 cups heavy cream
1 cup sour cream
   (optional)
½ to ¾ cup lime juice
   (optional)
   salt and pepper, to
   taste
24 lime slices, to
   garnish

In a stockpot, sweat the onions in the butter, covered, for 15 minutes or until soft. Add the tomatoes, chicken stock, tomato paste, sugar, thyme, and salt to taste, and simmer, covered, for 10 minutes. Puree.

To serve the soup cold: Add the cream, sour cream, lime juice, and salt and pepper to taste, and force through a fine sieve. Chill, and garnish with a slice of lime.

To serve hot: Add the cream, reheat, and serve garnished with a dollop of sour cream and a lime slice. Omit the lime juice.

YIELD: 24 servings

Cream of Tomato and Orange Soup

3 quarts tomato juice
3 quarts orange juice
1 quart chicken stock
1 cup sherry, or to taste
½ cup lemon juice

¼ cup sugar
1 quart plus one cup heavy
  cream, whipped
salt and pepper, to taste

In a stockpot, simmer the tomato juice, orange juice, chicken stock, sherry, lemon juice, and sugar for 10 minutes. Fold in 1 quart of the whipped cream, and season to taste with salt and pepper.

Ladle into bowls, and garnish with a dollop of the remaining whipped cream.

YIELD: 24 servings

Billi Bi
(Cream of Mussel Soup)

12 quarts mussels, scrubbed and bearded	¾ cup butter
1 quart dry white wine	pepper, to taste
12 shallots, minced	cayenne pepper, to taste
16 sprigs parsley	2 quarts heavy cream
2 teaspoons dried thyme	6 egg yolks
2 bay leaves	2 cups minced parsley

In a stockpot, place the mussels, wine, shallots, parsley, thyme, bay leaves, butter, and pepper to taste. Cover and bring to a boil. Simmer 5 minutes or until the mussels open.

Remove the mussels from their shells, and set aside for another use. (You can use some to garnish the soup.) Strain the cooking liquid into a pot, and bring to a boil. Season with cayenne and add 1 quart of the heavy cream.

Mix the egg yolks with the remaining cream and add to the soup. Heat until the soup is almost boiling and slightly thickened.

Serve hot or cold, garnished with minced parsley.

YIELD: 24 servings

NOTE: Billi Bi is one of the great soups of this world—startlingly delicious and subtle, yet simple to prepare. One source states that it was invented at Maxim's in Paris, but considering that it uses the liquid from Moules Marinière enriched with eggs and cream, I would not be surprised if it came out of the kitchen of a homemaker in Brittany or Normandy. Whatever its source, it is worth the extra effort involved in its preparation.

Potage Saint-Jacques
(Cream of Scallop Soup)

6 pounds scallops	1 teaspoon cayenne pepper
3 quarts dry white wine	salt and pepper, to taste
1 pound mushrooms, minced	1 quart heavy cream
¾ cup minced shallots	8 egg yolks
¾ cup butter	sherry, to taste
bunch of parsley	

In a pot, place the scallops, wine, mushrooms, shallots, butter, parsley, cayenne, and salt and pepper to taste. Bring just to a boil over medium heat. Remove the scallops. Simmer the liquid for 5 minutes more, and strain.

Bring the liquid back to a simmer, and make the liaison with the egg yolks and cream. Correct the seasoning with the sherry.

Serve garnished with some of the scallops.

YIELD: 24 servings

NOTE: Use the remaining scallops for another dish.

Try making this soup with shrimp (you can use just the shells). Or try lobster bodies, chopped. Simmer for about 10 minutes.

❧ CHEESE AND ❧ VEGETABLE SOUPS

Although the great surge in vegetarian cooking has diminished, no chef will want to be without a suitable selection of meatless soups to offer. Many of the vegetarian soups here are hearty and filling with a veritable garden of vegetables including beans or rice to make them complete meals. Others, such as the Snow Pea Soup, are as light and subtle as soup can be.

If you are not cooking for a vegetarian regimen, the meatless soups can often be made with chicken, veal, or beef stock to achieve a heartier flavor—though not necessarily to improve them, since these soups are superb as they stand. Of course, many of the soups are open to substitution. Use what is fresh rather than trying to force a particular selection of vegetables. It goes without saying that a tomato soup must have tomatoes, but if it calls for minced shallots and you have only scallions, do not be concerned. The very lack of a particular ingredient may well lead you to the foundation of a new soup, if not the new soup itself.

In preparing cheese soups be careful to add the cheese slowly and heat the soup gently. If you try to rush the process you can have a great glob of cheese that is virtually indissoluble.

Cheddar Cheese Soup

2 cups minced green peppers	2 cups flour
2 cups minced carrots	3 quarts chicken stock
2 cups minced onions	2 pounds grated Cheddar
2 cups minced celery	cheese
2 cups butter	3 quarts medium cream

In a pot, sweat the peppers, carrots, onions, and celery in the butter until soft but not brown. Stir in the flour and cook, stirring, for 5 minutes or until the mixture is foamy and just starts to turn golden.

Stir in the stock and cook, stirring until the soup reaches a boil and thickens.

Simmer 25 minutes. Lower the heat and stir in the cheese a handful at a time until it is melted. Stir in the cream and bring up to temperature. Do not boil.

YIELD: 24 servings

NOTE: The soup can be served hot or cold. If you want a soup of smoother texture, strain out the vegetables before adding the cheese.

Kaassoep
(Gouda Cheese Soup)

1½ cups butter	1 tablespoon Worcestershire
1½ cups flour	sauce
3 quarts half-and-half	Tabasco, to taste
3 quarts milk	salt, to taste
3 quarts grated Gouda	paprika, to garnish
cheese	

In a stockpot, melt the butter, stir in the flour, and cook for 5 minutes, stirring constantly. Stir in the half-and-half and the milk, and cook, stirring until the mixture thickens and becomes smooth.

In a processor, puree 1 quart of the cheese with 1 quart of the hot milk mixture. Repeat, using the remaining cheese and 2 more quarts of the hot milk mixture. Turn the cheese-and-milk mixture into the remaining soup and heat, stirring, until the soup is hot but not boiling.

Add the Worcestershire sauce. Correct the seasoning with Tabasco and salt.

Serve in heated bowls and sprinkle with paprika.

YIELD: 36 servings

Gruyère Soup

1 cup butter	2½ quarts grated Gruyère
1 cup flour	cheese
2 quarts milk	1 tablespoon Tabasco, or to
2 quarts chicken stock	taste
2 tablespoons Dijon mustard	sautéed croutons, to
	accompany

In a stockpot, melt the butter, stir in the flour, and cook for about 5 minutes, stirring constantly. Add the milk and chicken stock with the mustard and cook, stirring, until thickened and smooth. Simmer 10 minutes.

Stir in the cheese and Tabasco, and heat gently until the cheese is just melted. Serve with the croutons on the side.

YIELD: 24 servings

Swiss Cheese Soup

8 onions, chopped	3 quarts milk
¾ cup butter	6 cups grated Gruyère cheese
¾ cup flour	salt and pepper, to taste
6 cups beef stock	

In a pot, sauté the onions in the butter until golden. Stir in the flour and cook, stirring, for 5 minutes. Add the stock and cook, stirring, until it thickens and comes to a boil. Simmer 30 minutes. Stir in the milk and simmer 10 minutes longer. Remove from the heat and gradually stir in the cheese until melted. Correct the seasoning with salt and pepper.

YIELD: 24 servings

Soupe Jardinière
(Garden Soup)

1½ cups olive oil	2 quarts shredded cabbage
1 quart minced onions	10 quarts water
16 garlic cloves, minced	salt and pepper, to taste
4 teaspoons oregano	1 quart diced green beans
8 tomatoes, peeled, seeded, and chopped	1 quart diced zucchini
½ cup tomato paste	¾ cup minced parsley
2 quarts diced potatoes	2 quarts basil leaves
1 quart diced carrots	2⅔ cups grated Parmesan cheese
1 quart diced celery	

In a stockpot, heat ½ cup olive oil and sweat the onions and 8 minced garlic cloves with the oregano over medium heat until soft.

Add the tomatoes and tomato paste and simmer 5 minutes, stirring occasionally.

Add the potatoes, carrots, celery, cabbage, water, and salt and pepper to taste, and simmer for 1 hour.

Add the beans and zucchini and simmer 20 minutes longer.

Meanwhile, in a blender, puree the parsley, basil, remaining minced garlic cloves, and remaining olive oil until smooth. Blend in the cheese and season with salt and pepper.

To serve, ladle the soup into bowls and put a dollop of the basil mixture on each serving.

YIELD: 32 servings

Soupe Maraîchère
(Market Garden Soup)

1 quart minced onions	2 quarts shredded cabbage
1 quart sliced celery	1 quart shredded spinach
2 cups diced turnips	1 quart shredded lettuce
2 cups diced potatoes	7 quarts milk
¾ cup butter	salt and pepper, to taste
4 quarts chicken or beef stock	minced fresh chives, to garnish
2 cups fine noodles, broken into 1-inch lengths	minced fresh chervil, to garnish

In a stockpot, sweat the onions, celery, turnips, and potatoes in the butter, covered, until half cooked.

Add the stock and the noodles, and simmer until the vegetables and pasta are tender.

Add the cabbage, spinach, and lettuce, and simmer 5 minutes.

Stir in the milk, and season to taste with salt and pepper. Reheat.

Serve garnished with the chives and chervil.

YIELD: 24 servings

Soupe Menerboise

2 pounds zucchini, cubed	2 cups orzo or other small pasta
salt, to taste	
2 cups olive oil	8 tomatoes, peeled
8 onions, thinly sliced	salt and pepper, to taste
3 pounds tomatoes, chopped	12 garlic cloves
8 small potatoes, cubed	1 cup basil leaves
6 quarts hot water	8 egg yolks
2 cups shelled broad beans	1 cup Parmesan cheese

Sprinkle the zucchini with salt and drain 30 minutes in a colander.

In a stockpot, heat the olive oil and sweat the onions. Add the zucchini and cook 10 minutes longer. Add the chopped tomatoes and cook until they start to release their moisture. Add the potatoes and water and simmer 20 minutes or until the potatoes are almost cooked. Add the beans and pasta, and salt and pepper to taste.

In a processor, puree the remaining tomatoes, garlic, and basil until smooth. Add the egg yolks and process until the mixture resembles a thin mayonnaise.

When the pasta is tender, combine 1 quart of soup with the garlic-egg mixture and mix well. Add the mixture to the soup and heat gently, stirring until the soup is slightly thickened. Stir in the cheese.

If desired, serve additional cheese on the side.

YIELD: 24 servings

Minestrone di Romagna
(Italian Vegetable Soup)

1 quart sliced onions	4 quarts beef stock
2 cups olive oil	rind from 4 pounds Parmesan cheese (optional)
½ cup butter	
1 quart diced carrots	2⅔ cups canned plum tomatoes and their juice
1 quart diced celery	
2 quarts diced potatoes	salt, to taste
2 quarts diced zucchini	8 cups canned cannellini beans
1 quart diced green beans	
3 quarts shredded Savoy cabbage	2 cups grated Parmesan cheese

In a stockpot, sweat the onions in the oil and butter until golden. Add the carrots and cook for 5 minutes. Add the celery and cook for 2 minutes. Add the potatoes and cook for 2 minutes. Add the zucchini and cook for 2 minutes. Add the beans and cook for 2 minutes. Finally add the cabbage and cook for 5 minutes, stirring occasionally. Add the stock, the cheese rind (if using), the tomatoes with their juice, and salt to taste.

Cover and simmer gently for 1½ hours or until thickened and

rich in flavor. Discard the cheese rind and add the cannellini beans. Bring up to temperature. Serve the soup with the cheese on the side.

YIELD: 24 servings

Potage Printanier
(Spring Soup)

12 leeks, minced	1 cup rice
2 cups minced onions	4 pounds asparagus in 1-inch
½ cup butter	sections
8 potatoes, thinly sliced	2 pounds chopped spinach
4 carrots, thinly sliced	1 quart light cream
8 teaspoons salt	salt and pepper, to taste
6 quarts hot water	

In a stockpot, sauté the leeks and onions in the butter until soft but not brown.

Add the potatoes, carrots, salt, and 6 cups of hot water. Simmer covered for 15 minutes.

Add the rice and simmer 10 minutes. Add the asparagus and simmer 15 minutes longer. Add the spinach and simmer 5 minutes.

Stir in the cream and bring to a boil. Correct the seasoning with salt and pepper.

YIELD: 24 servings

Soupe de Légumes
_____(Pureed Vegetable Soup)_____

15 tomatoes, peeled, seeded, and chopped	bouquet garni of 1½ teaspoons rosemary, 1 teaspoon thyme, 3 bay leaves
6 onions, chopped	
6 carrots, chopped	
6 stalks celery, chopped	6 quarts chicken stock
6 potatoes, chopped	salt and pepper, to taste
6 leeks, chopped	24 toasted croûtes
½ bunch parsley, tied	3 cups grated Gruyère

In a stockpot, simmer the tomatoes, onions, carrots, celery, potatoes, leeks, parsley, bouquet garni, and chicken stock for 1 hour. Remove and discard the parsley and the bouquet garni.

Puree the soup and reheat. Correct the seasoning with salt and pepper to taste.

Serve garnished with the croûtes and pass the cheese separately.
YIELD: 24 servings

NOTE: The soup can be enriched by stirring in 1 quart of heavy cream. For further enrichment, stir in just enough dry sherry to heighten the flavor.

Soupe aux Légumes
_____(Soup with Vegetables)_____

¼ cup butter	1 quart diced green beans
1 cup olive oil	4 quarts chicken stock
8 onions, sliced	2 cups vermicelli, broken
8 turnips, shredded	salt and pepper, to taste
8 carrots, shredded	2 cups chopped spinach
8 parsnips, shredded	2 cups peas
4 stalks celery, thinly sliced	12 tomatoes, peeled and sliced

In a stockpot, heat the butter and oil and add the onions, turnips, carrots, parsnips, and celery, and cook, stirring, for 5 minutes. Add the beans and cook 3 minutes. Add the chicken stock and vermicelli, and season with salt and pepper.

Simmer about 15 minutes or until the vegetables are tender. Add the spinach, peas and, tomatoes, and cook until just tender. Correct the seasoning with salt and pepper.

YIELD: 24 servings

Black Bean Soup

1 pound black beans	3 leeks, trimmed and
water to cover	sliced
5 quarts cold water	2 bay leaves
3 stalks celery, chopped	4 teaspoons salt
3 large onions, chopped	1 teaspoon black pepper
½ cup butter	½ to 1 cup Madeira
3 tablespoons flour	3 hard-cooked eggs,
½ cup minced parsley	peeled and chopped
rind and bone of a smoked	24 lemon slices, to
ham, or 6 ham hocks	garnish

Wash the beans and soak overnight in water to cover. Drain and put into a stockpot with the 5 quarts of cold water. Simmer for 1½ hours.

In another pot, sweat the celery and onions in the butter until soft. Stir in the flour and parsley, and cook, stirring, for 5 minutes. Add 2 ladles of the beans' cooking liquid and bring to a boil, stirring. Return the mixture to the stock and add the ham bone and rind (or ham hocks), leeks, bay leaves, salt, and pepper. Simmer 4 hours.

Remove and discard the ham bones, rind, and bay leaves, saving the ham meat. Chop the meat into small dice. Force the soup through a food mill. Add the Madeira to taste and reheat the soup.

Fold in the chopped eggs and serve garnished with a lemon slice.

YIELD: 24 servings

Potage de Pois Chiches
(Chick Pea Soup)

2 pounds lean slab bacon,
  diced
3 quarts chopped leeks
¼ cup medium hot paprika
4 quarts cooked chick peas
  and their liquid

3 quarts beef stock
1½ quarts peeled, seeded,
  and chopped tomatoes
salt and pepper, to taste

In a stockpot, try out the bacon to render the fat. Add the leeks, cover, and sweat until softened. Stir in the paprika, and cook for 4 minutes.

Add the chick peas, their liquid, the beef stock, and the tomatoes. Simmer for 1 hour.

Correct the seasoning with salt and pepper, and carefully skim off any excess fat.

YIELD: 24 servings

Portuguese Chick Pea and Garlic Soup

6 cups stale bread with the
  crusts removed, cut into
  ½-inch cubes
2 cups olive oil
2 heads garlic, peeled
2 teaspoons salt

1½ cup minced fresh mint
1 cup minced parsley
6 quarts chicken stock
9 cups cooked chick peas
  mint sprigs, to garnish

In a skillet, sauté the bread cubes in 1 cup of the olive oil until golden. Drain on paper toweling and set aside.

In a processor, puree the garlic, salt, mint, and parsley, and add the second cup of olive oil a drop at a time.

In a large saucepan, bring the chicken stock and chick peas to a boil and simmer for 5 minutes. Transfer the garlic mixture to a

tureen and pour in the soup. Sprinkle with the croutons and garnish with the mint sprigs.
YIELD: 24 servings

Zöldbableves
(Green Bean Soup)

4 pounds green beans, cut
    into 1-inch pieces
4 quarts veal or chicken
    stock
2 tablespoons salt
4 garlic cloves
4 teaspoons vinegar
½ cup butter

4 onions, chopped
4 teaspoons paprika
½ cup minced parsley
½ cup flour
1 cup sour cream, at room
    temperature
salt and pepper, to taste

Simmer the green beans in boiling stock with the salt, garlic, and vinegar for 15 minutes or until almost tender. Remove from the heat.

In a saucepan, heat the butter and sauté the onion until it is soft but not brown. Add the paprika, parsley, and flour, and cook for about 3 minutes, stirring constantly.

Add 2 cups of the bean liquor to the roux, and stir until smooth. Add the mixture to the beans, and simmer 10 minutes longer or until the beans are tender. Let the soup cool for a few minutes, remove and discard the garlic.

Add some of the warm soup to the sour cream, mix, and return to the soup and reheat gently. Correct the seasoning with salt and pepper.
YIELD: 24 servings

Portuguese Red Bean Soup

1 quart dried red kidney beans	4 pounds potatoes, diced
12 onions, sliced	1½ cups tomato paste
8 garlic cloves, peeled and minced	8 bay leaves
1 cup bacon fat	2 tablespoons allspice
	salt and pepper, to taste

Soak the beans in water to cover for 12 to 24 hours. Drain.

Put the beans in a pot with cold water to cover and simmer 15 minutes. Drain.

In a skillet, sauté the onions and garlic in the bacon fat until golden. Add to the beans with the potatoes, tomato paste, bay leaves, and allspice.

Simmer for 3 hours, stirring often and adding more water as needed. Correct seasoning with salt and pepper.

YIELD: 24 servings

Lentil and Tomato Soup

2⅔ cups dried lentils	¾ cup minced parsley
4 quarts water	8 garlic cloves, minced
2 pounds carrots, chopped	1 teaspoon thyme
8 stalks celery, chopped	1 teaspoon tarragon
4 onions, chopped	½ teaspoon dill
1 quart tomato paste	salt and pepper, to taste
2 cups dry white wine	

In a stockpot, combine the lentils, water, carrots, celery, and onions.

Simmer 2 hours or until the lentils are tender. It may be necessary to add water as the mixture cooks to keep the vegetables covered.

Add the tomato paste, wine, parsley, garlic, thyme, tarragon, dill, and salt and pepper to taste. Simmer 20 minutes longer and correct seasoning.

YIELD: 24 servings

_____Mexican Lima Bean Soup with Salsa_____

2 pounds dried lima beans
  water, to cover
2 large onions, chopped
4 tablespoons oil
5 pounds canned tomatoes,
  chopped, with tomato
  liquid

salsa verde (see recipe,
  below)
salt, to taste
crumbled corn chips, to
  garnish

Soak the beans in water to cover overnight. Slip the skins off the beans and simmer the beans in water to cover by 1 inch until tender, about 30 minutes. Puree the beans. (If you wish to be lazy about this, you can remove the skins by simmering the soaked beans until they are tender, then forcing them through a food mill.)

In a skillet, sauté the onions in the oil until golden and add to the bean puree along with the tomatoes and their liquid. Add the salsa verde and correct the seasoning with salt if needed. Simmer about 30 minutes longer.

Serve topped with crumbled corn chips.

_____Salsa Verde (Green Sauce)_____

¾ pound tomatillos, chopped
1 onion, chopped
4 serrano or jalapeño chiles

2 cloves garlic, chopped
½ bunch coriander, chopped
  salt and pepper, to taste

In a processor combine the tomatillos, onion, chiles, garlic, and coriander, and process until coarsely chopped. Correct seasoning with salt and pepper.

Bableves
(Hungarian Bean Soup)

2 pounds dried navy or pea beans	½ cup chopped onion
water, to cover	½ cup vegetable oil
4 teaspoons salt	4 teaspoons paprika
4 carrots	½ cup flour
4 leeks	¼ cup minced parsley
4 garlic cloves, peeled	1 cup sour cream (optional)
4 ham hocks	3 tablespoons vinegar
water, to cover	salt and pepper, to taste

Soak the beans overnight in water to cover. Drain and rinse the beans and put them into a stockpot with the salt, carrots, leeks, garlic, ham hocks, and enough water to cover by 2 inches. Simmer partially covered for 2½ to 3 hours or until the beans are tender, adding more water as needed. Discard the garlic cloves. Remove the ham hocks, discard the bones, and dice and reserve the meat.

In a saucepan, sauté the onion in the oil until soft. Stir in the paprika and then the flour, and let it froth for about 3 minutes. Add the parsley, and thin with 2 cups of stock from the soup.

Slowly pour the liquid roux into the soup and simmer 20 minutes. If the soup is too thick, add more water.

Add some of the soup to the sour cream to warm it, and slowly stir the mixture into the soup. (This step may be omitted.) Add vinegar and correct the seasoning with salt and pepper.

Add the meat to the soup and reheat gently.

YIELD: 24 servings

Caldo Gallego
(Galician White Bean Soup)

3 quarts dried white beans
12 quarts water
4 tablespoons salt
4½ pounds ham, diced
4½ quarts veal or chicken
stock
3 quarts additional stock, or
as needed
½ cup minced salt pork
12 garlic cloves, chopped

1 tablespoon salt
3 pounds potatoes, cut into
¾-inch cubes
9 turnips, cut into ½-inch
cubes
1½ quarts cooked collard
greens
1½ cups olive oil
salt and pepper, to taste

Soak the beans in the water and salt overnight. Drain the beans, and put into a stockpot with the ham and stock and bring to a boil, skimming the scum from the surface.

Lower the heat and simmer the mixture, covered, for 50 minutes, adding additional stock as needed to cover the beans.

In a processor, puree the salt pork, garlic, and salt. Add to the soup with the potatoes and turnips, and simmer 10 minutes longer. Add the collard greens and olive oil, and simmer 5 minutes longer or until the potatoes are tender.

Scoop 1½ cups of the bean mixture from the soup, and puree. Return the puree to the soup, and correct the seasoning with salt and pepper.

YIELD: 24 servings

Soupe de Tullins
_____(Bean and Sorrel Soup)_____

8 carrots, minced
8 leeks, minced
12 onions, minced
¼ cup butter
1 quart cooked white beans
8 tomatoes, peeled, seeded, and quartered
6 quarts chicken or veal stock

4 bunches sorrel, about 2 pounds
3 cups heavy cream
salt and pepper, to taste
toasted croûtes, to garnish

In a stockpot, sauté the carrots, leeks, and onions in the butter until golden. Cover, and simmer the vegetables for 20 minutes in their juices. Add the beans, tomatoes, and stock, and simmer 1 hour.

In a skillet, stew the sorrel in its own juice until wilted. Add to the soup 15 minutes before serving. Add the cream to the soup and heat through. Puree the soup. Adjust seasoning with salt and pepper to taste.

Serve with toasted croûtes on the side.
YIELD: 24 servings

Spárgaleves
_____(Asparagus Soup)_____

4 pounds asparagus cut into 1-inch pieces
4 quarts veal or chicken stock
4 teaspoons sugar
2 tablespoons salt

½ cup butter
½ cup flour
½ cup minced parsley
2 cups milk
galuska (see recipe, below)

Simmer the asparagus in stock, sugar, and salt for 5 minutes. In a saucepan, melt the butter, stir in the flour and parsley, and cook for 5 minutes or until foaming. Dilute the roux with the milk and then add the asparagus mixture and correct the seasoning. Simmer for 5 minutes or until the asparagus is cooked.

Add the cooked galuska (dumplings) just before serving.
YIELD: 24 servings

Galuska
(Hungarian Soft Dumplings)

4 cups sifted flour
2 teaspoons salt
4 eggs
  cold water as needed
3 tablespoons butter

In a processor, combine the flour, salt, and eggs, and process until combined.

With the machine running, add enough cold water to hold the dough together, about ⅔ to ¾ cup. Process until the dough separates from the side of the bowl. Let rest for 45 minutes.

Bring a large pot of salted water to a boil. Turn the mixture onto a wet board. Using the back of a knife or the edge of a soupspoon, scrape ½-inch knobs of the dough into the water. The galuska are done as soon as they rise to the surface. With a skimmer remove them from the surface and place in a bowl with the butter. Continue the process with the remaining mixture. Toss the dumplings gently with the butter to coat them evenly and keep warm until ready to use.

NOTE: You can use a spaetzle maker or chestnut roaster to shape the galuska. If the food mill has a blade with large holes, you can force the mixture through it.

Broccoli and Macaroni Soup

½ cup minced fat salt pork
6 quarts water
¾ cup tomato paste
¼ cup olive oil
4 cloves garlic, minced
1 tablespoon salt

1 teaspoon pepper
3 quarts broccoli florets
2 pounds elbow macaroni
  grated Parmesan cheese, to
  accompany

In a stockpot, sauté the pork until brown. Add the water, tomato paste, olive oil, garlic, salt, and pepper. Simmer 20 minutes.

Add the broccoli, and simmer 5 minutes. Add the macaroni, and cook 10 minutes or until just tender.

Serve with cheese on the side.

YIELD: 24 servings

Karfiolleves
(Hungarian Cauliflower Soup)

4 heads cauliflower
6 quarts veal or chicken
  stock
1 tablespoon salt
½ cup butter

½ cup flour
⅓ cup minced parsley
2 cups sour cream, room
  temperature
  salt and pepper, to taste

Cut the cauliflower heads into florets, place in a stockpot with the stock and salt, and simmer about 7 minutes or until tender but still crisp.

In a saucepan, make a roux with the butter, flour, and parsley. Thin it with 2 cups of cooking liquid from cauliflower. Pour the roux into the soup, and simmer 10 minutes or until the cauliflower is tender and the soup has lost all floury taste.

Stir 1 cup of soup into the sour cream, and return the mixture to the soup. Heat gently without boiling. Correct the seasoning with salt and pepper.

YIELD: 24 servings

Celery and Apple Soup

½ cup butter
¾ cup peanut oil
8 stalks celery, sliced
4 onions, sliced
4 carrots, sliced
24 Cortland apples, peeled
   and sliced

2 quarts chicken stock
4 teaspoons meat glaze
  salt and pepper, to taste
  flour for dredging

In a stockpot, melt the butter with 4 tablespoons of oil. Sweat the celery, onions, and carrots slowly until wilted. Add 20 sliced apples and cook until soft but not brown. Add the chicken stock and meat glaze. Season with salt and pepper, and simmer 5 minutes. Puree. Return to the pan and reheat.

Dust the remaining apple slices with the flour, and sauté in the remaining oil until golden on both sides. Serve the soup garnished with apple rings.

YIELD: 24 servings

NOTE: It is best to cook the apple rings just before serving.

Sopa de Elote
(Mexican Corn Soup)

4 onions, minced
½ pound butter
2½ quarts cooked corn
12 tomatoes, peeled and
   seeded

4 quarts beef stock
  salt and pepper, to taste
1 quart heavy cream

In a skillet, sauté the onion in the butter until soft.

Puree 2 quarts of the corn with the onion and tomatoes and enough stock to make a smooth puree. In a stockpot, combine the ingredients with the remaining stock, and heat. Correct seasoning with salt and pepper.

Add the cream, stirring, and reheat without boiling. Serve garnished with the remaining corn.
YIELD: 24 servings

Cucumber Soup

12 cucumbers, peeled, seeded, and cut in 2-inch lengths	salt and pepper, to taste
4 leeks, split lengthwise	2 cups yogurt, crème fraîche, or sour cream
4 quarts chicken stock	
1 quart raw spinach leaves	4 small cucumbers, scored, to garnish
4 teaspoons minced dill	
4 teaspoons minced chervil	dill sprigs, to garnish

In a stockpot, simmer the cucumber and leeks in the stock for 30 minutes. Puree in a processor, add the spinach, and puree again. Return to the pot, and season with dill, chervil, salt, and pepper.

Serve hot or cold with a generous dollop of yogurt, crème fraîche, or sour cream. Thinly slice the scored cucumbers, and garnish the soup with cucumber slices and dill sprigs.
YIELD: 24 servings

Potage Arlesienne
(Eggplant and Vegetable Soup)

4 pounds eggplant, peeled and cut in 1-inch cubes	salt and pepper, to taste
1 cup peanut oil	4 bay leaves
6 cups chopped onions	2 teaspoons dried thyme
4 tablespoons minced garlic	3 quarts chopped tomatoes
½ cup butter	1 cup rice
	4 quarts chicken stock

In a skillet, heat the oil almost to the smoking point and add the eggplant. Cook, stirring, until lightly browned; if necessary cook in batches. Drain the cubes.

In a stockpot, sweat the onion and garlic in the butter, and add the eggplant, salt, pepper, bay leaves, and thyme. Cook 1 minute. Add the tomatoes, rice, and stock, and simmer 20 minutes.

Discard the bay leaves. Puree the soup, and return it to the pot and reheat.

YIELD: 24 servings

Zuppa di Scarola alla Siciliana
(Sicilian Escarole Soup)

4 pounds escarole	1 quart diced, cooked chicken
1 pound lean, sliced bacon	salt and pepper, to taste
4 teaspoons olive oil	grated Parmesan cheese, to
8 garlic cloves, crushed	accompany
8 quarts chicken stock	
1 pound broken vermicelli or melon seed pasta (see Note)	

Wash and drain the escarole and cut it into ¼-inch shreds.

In a skillet, sauté the bacon in the oil until cooked but not crisp. Remove the bacon, drain it, and cut it into small squares.

In the same skillet, sauté the garlic in the remaining fat until golden but not brown.

In a pot, simmer the garlic, bacon, stock, and escarole uncovered for 10 minutes. Add the pasta and cook 10 minutes longer. Add the chicken. Correct the seasoning with salt and pepper.

To serve, pass the Parmesan cheese separately.

YIELD: 24 servings

NOTE: There are dozens of small, shaped pastas, such as orzo (rice), farina, stellae (stars), semi di melone (melon seed), tiny shells, and so on. Use whichever you prefer.

Soupe à l'Ail
_____(Garlic Soup)_____

2 cups unpeeled garlic cloves	nutmeg, to taste
8 tablespoons butter	cayenne pepper, to taste
1 cup olive oil	24 slices toasted French bread
4 quarts chicken stock	¼ cup minced parsley, to
24 egg yolks	garnish
2 teaspoons salt	

Blanch the garlic for 1 minute in boiling water to cover. Drain, and pinch off the skins.

In a stockpot, heat the butter and ¼ cup of olive oil and sweat the garlic until very soft without letting it brown. Add the stock and simmer 20 minutes.

In a bowl, beat the eggs and beat in the remaining ¾ cup of oil, a little at a time, until the mixture is as thick as mayonnaise. Add 1 cup of the soup liquid and mix well. Return the mixture to the hot soup in a slow, steady stream. Heat almost to the boiling point.

Strain, mashing the garlic. Correct the seasoning with the salt, nutmeg, and cayenne pepper.

Place the toasted bread in a tureen and pour on the hot soup. Sprinkle with parsley and serve.

YIELD: 24 servings

Sopa de Ajo
_____(Spicy Garlic Soup)_____

2 cups olive oil	1 teaspoon cayenne pepper
½ cup minced garlic	4 teaspoons salt
3 quarts crumbled French bread without crusts	8 eggs, lightly beaten
4 teaspoons paprika	¼ cup minced parsley, to garnish
6 quarts water	

In a saucepan, heat the olive oil over low heat. Add the garlic and cook, stirring, for 2 to 3 minutes, or until it is very soft but not brown.

Stir in the breadcrumbs, and raise the heat. Cook, stirring, until the bread is golden; be careful not to burn the garlic. Stir in the paprika, water, cayenne, and salt. Simmer uncovered for 30 minutes.

Strain the soup and mash the bread until pulpy. Return the pulp to the soup and slowly beat in the eggs. Reheat to just below boiling point. Correct the seasoning with salt and cayenne pepper.

Serve sprinkled with the parsley.

YIELD: 24 servings

Karalábéleves
(Kohlrabi Soup)

4 pounds kohlrabi	salt and pepper, to taste
2 cups vegetable oil	4 quarts veal or chicken stock
½ cup flour	1 cup sour cream
½ cup minced parsley	

Peel the kohlrabi and cut into ½-inch dice.

In a stockpot, sauté the kohlrabi pieces in the oil until golden. Sprinkle with the flour, and cook, stirring, until lightly browned. Add the parsley, salt, and pepper, and stir in the stock.

Simmer partially covered for 45 minutes or until the kohlrabi is tender. Let the soup cool for a few minutes and use some of the broth to dilute the sour cream. Add the sour-cream mixture to the soup and reheat gently.

YIELD: 24 servings

_____Leek and Vermicelli Soup_____

24 leeks, chopped	1 teaspoon pepper
1 cup butter	½ cup flour
½ pound vermicelli	water
4 quarts chicken stock	1 cup milk
salt, to taste	

In a pot, sweat the leeks in the butter until soft but not brown. Break the vermicelli into 1- to 2-inch lengths, and add to the pot with the chicken stock, salt, and pepper. Cover and simmer 10 minutes.

In a bowl, combine the flour and enough water to make a thin slurry. Stir into the soup, whisking constantly. Add the milk and heat until hot and slightly thickened.

YIELD: 24 servings

Soupe à la Santé
_____(Healthy Soup)_____

1 quart minced celery	¼ cup minced fresh chervil
1 cup thinly sliced scallions	5 quarts chicken stock
½ pound butter	salt and pepper, to taste
4 heads Boston lettuce,	sugar (as needed)
shredded	grated Parmesan cheese, to
4 pounds sorrel, shredded	accompany

In a stockpot, sweat the celery and scallions in the butter until softened.

Add the lettuce, sorrel, and chervil, and cook, stirring, for about 10 minutes. Add the chicken stock and simmer for 30 minutes. Correct the seasonings with salt and pepper and a little sugar if too acidic.

To serve, pass the cheese separately.

YIELD: 24 servings

Lettuce and Rice Soup

2 quarts minced scallions
1 cup butter
¾ cup flour
6 quarts chicken stock
3 cups cooked rice

2 quarts shredded Boston
  lettuce
1 quart shelled peas
salt and pepper, to taste

In a stockpot, sweat the scallions in the butter until soft but not brown. Stir in the flour, and cook for 2 minutes. Add the stock, stirring constantly until smooth. Add the rice, heat to boiling, and add the lettuce and peas. Simmer, covered, until the peas are cooked, about 5 minutes. Correct the seasoning with salt and pepper.
YIELD: 24 servings

NOTE: If you are using frozen peas, they will be done as soon as the soup returns to the boil.

Gombaleves
(Hungarian Mushroom Soup)

4 onions, minced
1 cup lard or vegetable oil
2 pounds mushrooms, sliced
6 quarts beef stock
1 tablespoon salt

pepper, to taste
½ cup flour
½ cup minced parsley
2 cups sour cream

In a stockpot, sauté the onions in ½ cup of the lard or oil until soft but not brown. Add the mushrooms and cook until tender. Add the stock, scraping up any browned bits, season with the salt and pepper, and simmer 5 minutes.

In a saucepan, heat the remaining lard or oil and add the flour. Cook 3 minutes, stirring, then add the parsley.

Pour some of the hot soup into the flour mixture and cook, stirring, to make a liquid roux. Turn the roux into the hot soup, and simmer, partially covered, for 20 minutes. Correct the seasoning with salt and pepper.

Add some of the hot soup to the sour cream to warm it, and turn it into the soup. Heat gently without boiling.

YIELD: 24 servings

Mushroom Soup

2 pounds mushrooms	salt and pepper, to taste
8 onions, minced	¼ cup rice
¾ cup butter	4 bay leaves
½ cup flour	½ cup minced watercress, to
5 quarts chicken stock	garnish

Mince the mushroom stems and slice the caps.

In a stockpot, sweat the mushrooms and onions in ½ cup butter until soft.

Remove from the heat and add the remaining butter. Stir in the flour, and cook until the mixture thickens slightly. Add the stock and season with salt and pepper. Bring to a boil, stirring occasionally. Add the rice and bay leaves and simmer 15 to 20 minutes. Discard the bay leaves and correct the seasoning. Sprinkle with the watercress to garnish.

YIELD: 24 servings

Mushroom and Barley Soup I

12 ounces dried Polish mushrooms	6½ quarts chicken or veal stock
1½ quarts hot water	4 teaspoons salt
4 onions, chopped	1 teaspoon pepper
4 leeks, chopped	8 potatoes, diced
¾ cup butter	4 bay leaves
4 carrots, diced	1 quart sour cream
1⅓ cups barley	minced dill, to garnish

Soak the mushrooms in the water for 20 minutes. Drain, reserving the liquid and the mushrooms. Chop the mushrooms and set aside. Strain the liquid and set aside.

In a stockpot, sweat the onions and leeks in the butter until soft. Add the carrots, barley, mushroom liquid, stock, salt, and pepper, and simmer, covered, for 1 hour. Add the potatoes, bay leaves, and mushrooms, and cook the soup, covered, for 20 minutes. Discard the bay leaves, and stir in the sour cream. Reheat gently without boiling. Garnish each serving with the dill.

YIELD: 24 servings

NOTE: This soup calls for Polish mushrooms, which are wild mushrooms that have been dried and are used often in Middle European cookery. You can substitute other dried mushrooms, but the flavor will not be the same. Dried chanterelles make a good substitute, but the Asian mushrooms have a completely different flavor and are not recommended.

Mushroom and Barley Soup II

3 pounds beef bones	¾ cup lard
3 carrots, sliced	3 cups pearl barley
6 stalks celery, sliced	1 quart minced onion
4 pounds chicken backs and necks	6 cups thinly sliced mushrooms
12 quarts water	½ cup minced parsley
¼ cup salt	12 dried mushrooms, broken up
2 teaspoons black pepper	

In a stockpot, simmer the beef bones, carrots, celery, chicken parts, water, salt, and pepper for 3 hours.

In a skillet, melt half the lard and sauté 1½ cups of the barley until it turns yellow and starts to make a crackling sound. Add the onion and cook, stirring, until it is limp and glossy.

Melt the remaining lard in another skillet, and sauté the mushrooms with the parsley. Set aside.

Strain the broth and discard the bones and vegetables. Add the remaining uncooked barley to the broth. Add the dried mushrooms, and simmer for 30 minutes.

Add the sautéed barley, and simmer 30 minutes. Add the sautéed mushrooms, and simmer 20 minutes longer.

Let stand, covered, for 30 minutes or longer before serving.
YIELD: 24 servings

Pilzensuppe
(German Mushroom Soup)

3 large onions, thinly sliced	2 tablespoons Worcestershire
1½ cups butter	sauce
6 tablespoons flour	salt and pepper, to taste
6 quarts beef stock	
3 pounds mushrooms, chopped	

In a stockpot, sauté the onions in the butter until they turn golden. Add the flour and cook for 3 minutes, stirring. Add the stock and mushrooms, and simmer for 10 minutes. Add the Worcestershire sauce, and correct the seasoning with salt and pepper.
YIELD: 24 servings

Carolina Okra Soup

5 pounds beef shanks	4 pounds tomatoes, peeled and chopped
6 marrow bones	
4 quarts cold water	2 hot peppers, chopped
3 pounds okra, sliced	pepper, to taste
2 onions, chopped	2 to 3 cups hot, cooked rice, to accompany
salt, to taste	
2 bay leaves	

In a stockpot, bring the beef shanks, marrow bones, and cold water to a boil. Skim off the scum. When scum ceases to rise, simmer very gently for 2 hours.

Add the okra, onions, salt, and bay leaves, and simmer for another hour or until the meat is very tender. Remove the bay leaves and discard.

Remove the shanks and marrow bones from the pot, and let them cool slightly.

Dice the meat and marrow and return to the kettle with the tomatoes and hot peppers. Simmer, covered, for 2 hours. Correct the seasoning with salt and pepper.

Serve the soup and pass the rice separately.

YIELD: 24 servings

Soupe aux Oignons
(Onion Soup)

4 quarts sliced onions	salt and pepper, to taste
¾ cup butter	24 slices French bread
6 quarts chicken or beef stock	

In a stockpot, sweat the onions in the butter until golden, stirring occasionally. Add the stock, and salt and pepper to taste. Simmer 20 minutes. Add the bread slices and simmer 5 minutes longer.

YIELD: 24 servings

Ouliat Tourri, or Toulia
(Onion Soup from Béarn)

2 cups olive oil	salt and pepper, to taste
48 slices French bread	16 egg yolks
1 quart minced onions	2 pounds grated Gruyère
2 cups flour	cheese
8 quarts beef stock	1⅓ cups Cognac or Armagnac

Make sautéed croûtes with half of the oil and the bread. Set aside.

Pour the remaining oil into a stockpot with the onions, and sweat the onions until they start to turn golden. Sprinkle with the flour and cook, stirring, for 5 minutes.

Add 2 quarts of stock, and bring to a boil, stirring. Add the remaining stock, and return to a boil. Simmer, covered, for 20 minutes. Force through a food mill. Correct the seasoning with salt and pepper.

In a tureen, beat the egg yolks with half of the grated cheese. Stir in the soup, a cup at a time.

Flame the Cognac or Armagnac. When the flames die out, add to the soup. Sprinkle with the remaining cheese and serve with the croûtes.

YIELD: 24 servings

NOTE: This onion soup from the region of Béarn in Southwest France has several regional names, as you can see from the original titles. It should not, however, be confused with the rich butter, egg, and tarragon sauce served over grilled meats and fish, which was created in a small restaurant outside of Paris.

Thourins (also Tourin and Torrin)
_____(Onion Soup from the Bordelaise)_____

12 large onions	6 quarts boiling beef stock
½ cup olive oil	48 slices stale rye bread
¼ cup flour	2⅔ cups grated Gruyère
2 cups dry white wine	cheese

In a stockpot, sauté the onions in the oil until golden brown but not burned.

Add the flour and cook, stirring, for 3 minutes. Add the wine and the boiling stock, and bring to a boil, stirring. Simmer for 20 minutes.

In a soup tureen or individual soup cups make a layer of bread slices and sprinkle with Gruyère. Continue layering, ending with the cheese. Pour the soup over the top and let stand for a few minutes before serving.

YIELD: 24 servings

Tourain Périgourdin
_____(Onion Soup from Southwest France)_____

¾ cup goose fat	salt and pepper, to taste
2 heads garlic	8 eggs
2 quarts thinly sliced onions	4 teaspoons red wine vinegar
½ cup flour	¾ cup minced parsley
1 #10 can tomatoes, undrained	24 slices toasted bread

In a kettle, melt the fat, add the garlic and onions, and cook until soft but not brown. Add the flour and cook, stirring, until it starts to turn golden. Add the tomatoes and cook, stirring occasionally, for about 20 minutes. Correct the seasoning with salt and pepper. Puree.

In a tureen, blend the eggs, vinegar, and parsley. Slowly stir in the hot soup, cover with the toast, and serve.
YIELD: 24 servings

Mediterranean Onion Soup

5 quarts thinly sliced onion	4 teaspoons dried thyme
4 teaspoons salt	3 teaspoons dried oregano
4 teaspoons sugar	4 bay leaves
2 teaspoons pepper	1 #10 can Italian tomatoes
¾ cup olive oil	¾ cup tomato paste
12 garlic cloves, crushed	5 quarts chicken stock
½ bunch parsley sprigs, tied together	2 cups ditalini or other soup pasta

In a stockpot, sauté the onions, salt, sugar, and pepper in the oil until the onions are golden. Partially cover, and cook until very soft but not burned.

Stir in the garlic, parsley, thyme, oregano, and bay leaves, and cook 2 minutes.

Drain the tomatoes, puree, and strain out the seeds. Stir the puree into the onion mixture, and add the tomato paste and stock. Simmer, partially covered, for 30 minutes. Correct the seasoning, and add the pasta. Simmer until tender. Discard the bay leaves and parsley sprigs.
YIELD: 24 servings

NOTE: You can pass grated Parmesan cheese with the soup, or grated Gruyère, or even the tomato, garlic, and basil mixture used in the Soupe Menerboise (see page 61).

Zweibelcreme Suppe
(Swiss Creamed Onion Soup)

24 slices whole-grain rye bread	pinch pepper
1¼ cups butter	pinch nutmeg
8 quarts thinly sliced onions	3 quarts milk
½ cup olive oil	3 quarts light cream
¾ teaspoon salt	12 egg yolks
	8 eggs
	minced chives, to garnish

Cut the bread into ¼-inch cubes. Sauté the bread cubes in 1 cup butter until golden and drain on toweling.

In a stockpot, sweat the onions in the remaining butter and the oil until very soft and just starting to turn golden, about 30 minutes. Season with salt, pepper, and nutmeg. Add the milk and cream and simmer, stirring occasionally, for 10 minutes.

In a bowl, beat the egg yolks and eggs and stir in 1 quart of hot soup. Return the mixture slowly to the soup, and cook over low heat until thickened.

Serve garnished with the sautéed bread cubes and chives.
YIELD: 24 servings

Potage Provençal
(Vegetable Soup Provençal)

4 pounds potatoes, sliced	4 quarts cold water
8 large onions, sliced	4 teaspoons salt
12 celery stalks, sliced	8 teaspoons pepper
8 leeks, sliced	4 pounds spinach
2 cups butter	2 cups light cream, scalded

In a stockpot, mix the potatoes, onions, celery, leeks, butter, water, salt, and pepper. Simmer until the potatoes are mushy, about 45 minutes.

Remove from the heat and stir in the spinach. Force the soup through a food mill.

Return to the pot and stir in the cream. Thin the soup with water, milk, or cream. It should be fairly thick.

YIELD: 24 servings

Soupe Bonne Femme
(Hot Potato Soup)

16 leeks, diced	8 teaspoons salt
4 onions, sliced	2 quarts hot milk
4 tablespoons butter	¼ cup butter
4 pounds potatoes, diced	¼ cup minced parsley, to
4 quarts hot water	garnish

In a stockpot, sweat the leeks and onions in the 4 tablespoons butter until soft but not brown. Add the potatoes, water, and salt, and simmer until the potatoes are soft.

Force soup through a food mill. Add the milk and the ¼ cup butter. Reheat and serve hot, garnished with the parsley.

YIELD: 24 servings

Caldo Verde
(Dilled Potato and Onion Soup)

24 potatoes, peeled and diced	4 cups minced dill
6 onions, minced	½ cup olive oil
2 heads of garlic, minced	salt and pepper, to taste
2 tablespoons salt	1 pound sliced bacon,
7½ quarts cold water	cooked and crumbled, to garnish

In a stockpot, simmer the potatoes, onions, garlic, salt, and water for 30 minutes. Add the dill and simmer 15 minutes longer. Puree, and stir in the olive oil and salt and pepper to taste. Serve garnished with the crumbled bacon.

For a less formal effect, mash the potatoes coarsely and puree the remaining soup. Combine the potatoes and pureed soup.
YIELD: 24 servings

Country Potato Soup

12 slices bacon, diced
12 leeks, trimmed and thinly
    sliced
6 potatoes, peeled and sliced

2 quarts chicken stock,
    approximately
    salt and pepper, to taste
2 cups sour cream

In a stockpot, sauté the bacon until most of the fat is rendered and the bacon is just starting to crisp. Drain off all but ½ cup of the fat. Add the leeks and sweat until soft. Add the potatoes, chicken stock, salt, and pepper, and simmer until the potatoes are very tender, about 30 minutes. Puree the soup.

If the soup is too thick, add chicken stock to thin. Stir in the sour cream and reheat but do not boil.
YIELD: 18 servings

Soupe de l'Ubac
(Potato Soup from Savoie)

8 pounds potatoes, quartered
8 quarts water
2 quarts milk
4 veal bones (optional)
    salt and pepper, to taste
¾ cup butter, in 1-tablespoon
    pieces

1 pound grated Gruyère
    cheese
24 slices stale French bread, to
    garnish

In a stockpot, simmer the potatoes, water, and milk with the veal bones and salt and pepper to taste for 40 minutes. Discard the veal bones.

Force the soup through a food mill. Return the soup to a kettle, and simmer 10 minutes longer.

Put the butter and cheese in a heated tureen, and pour on the hot soup. Garnish with the bread slices.

YIELD: 24 servings

Risi e Bisi, or
Minestra di Risi e Piselli
(Rice and Peas in Broth)

1 pound butter	salt and pepper, to taste
½ cup olive oil	5 cups Arborio rice
16 pounds fresh peas	6 quarts chicken stock
4 onions, minced	1⅓ cups grated Parmesan
½ cup minced parsley	cheese, to accompany
½ pound minced prosciutto	

Shell peas and set aside.

In a stockpot, melt the butter in the olive oil and add the peas, onions, parsley, prosciutto, salt, and pepper. Cook over low heat until peas are just tender. Add the rice and mix well.

Add 2 cups of stock to the mixture and cook, stirring, until the liquid evaporates. Continue adding the liquid 2 cups at a time, stirring often, until the rice is tender but not mushy. Stir in any remaining stock.

Serve immediately in soup dishes. Pass the cheese separately.

YIELD: 24 servings

NOTE: Arborio rice is a short, fat-grained Italian rice; it is mandatory for this dish. If desired, you can add more chicken stock to make this soupier. However, the soup should be very thick, though not so thick that it could be served as a rice dish.

Soupe de Riz à la Provençale
(Rice Soup Provençal)

3 cups chopped leeks	8 sprigs thyme
½ cup olive oil	12 sprigs parsley
1 cup flour	4 cloves garlic
7 quarts beef stock	salt and pepper, to taste
4 pounds tomatoes, peeled, seeded, and chopped	1 cup raw rice
4 stalks celery	½ pound minced salt pork, to garnish
4 bay leaves	

In a stockpot sweat the leeks in the oil until soft but not brown. Add the flour, and cook, stirring, for 2 minutes. Stir in the stock and bring to a boil.

Add the tomatoes. Make a faggot of the celery, bay leaves, thyme, and parsley. Add to the soup with the garlic, salt, and pepper. Simmer 15 minutes. Add the rice and simmer 15 minutes longer or until the rice is tender, stirring occasionally.

Meanwhile, fry the minced salt pork in a skillet until crisp. Drain on paper toweling. Discard the faggot from the soup.

Serve the soup garnished with the pork cubes.

YIELD: 24 servings

NOTE: If desired, you may garnish also with croutons.

Soupe aux Mange-touts I
(Snow Pea Soup I)

7 quarts chicken stock	½ cup minced gingerroot
8 tablespoons coriander leaves	1 pound snow peas, julienned

In a stockpot, simmer the chicken stock, coriander, and ginger for 10 minutes. Strain.

Bring the stock to a boil and add the snow peas. Turn off the heat and let stand 1 minute.

Serve at once.

YIELD: 24 servings

NOTE: Should be served immediately.

Soupe aux Mange-touts II
(Snow Pea Soup II)

2 cups minced onion	1 quart milk
4 garlic cloves, minced	¼ cup grated gingerroot
1 cup butter	salt and pepper, to
1 cup flour	taste
3 quarts chicken stock	24 to 48 pea pods, blanched,
4 pounds snow peas	to garnish

In a stockpot, sweat the onions and garlic in the butter until soft but not brown. Stir in the flour, and cook, stirring, for 3 minutes.

Add the stock, and cook, stirring, until it reaches a boil and is thickened.

Add the snow peas, and cook 5 minutes or until they are puffed and bright green. Pour in the milk, and simmer 3 minutes longer.

Puree, and strain into a clean stockpot. Add the gingerroot and salt and pepper to taste.

Reheat and serve garnished with 1 or 2 pea pods.

YIELD: 24 servings

Paparot
_____(Spinach and Cornmeal Soup, Friuli Style)_____

8 pounds spinach, stripped
   of stems
4 cloves garlic, peeled
½ cup butter
½ cup olive oil

8 quarts chicken or beef stock
   salt and pepper, to taste
1 quart cornmeal
2 cups sifted flour

In a stockpot, cook the spinach until wilted; use only the water left on the leaves after washing. Drain and squeeze out the excess water. Mince.

In a stockpot, cook the garlic in the butter and oil until golden. Discard the garlic. Add the spinach and the stock, and simmer 10 minutes. Correct the seasoning with the salt and pepper.

In a bowl mix the cornmeal and flour.

Remove 1 quart of liquid from the soup and let cool 5 minutes. Stir the cooled liquid into the flour-cornmeal mixture until there are no lumps. Add to the soup, stirring constantly until the soup is thick and smooth. Simmer 30 minutes.

YIELD: 24 servings

_____Squash and Corn Soup_____

6 quarts chicken stock
8 small summer squash, sliced
4 leeks, sliced
4 green peppers, sliced
4 large garlic cloves, minced
1 teaspoon thyme

12 slices fresh ginger
   salt, to taste
1 quart corn kernels
   grated Parmesan cheese, to
    garnish

In a stockpot, simmer the chicken stock, squash, leeks, peppers, garlic, thyme, ginger, and salt for about 1 hour. Add the corn and simmer 5 minutes longer.

Serve sprinkled with grated Parmesan cheese.

YIELD: 24 servings

Fresh Tomato Soup with Basil

12 tomatoes, chopped	2 bay leaves
4 carrots, sliced	¼ cup tomato paste
1 leek, sliced	5 quarts chicken stock
4 shallots, sliced	4 teaspoons salt
4 cloves garlic, sliced	pepper, to taste
½ cup olive oil	4 cups fresh basil leaves
4 sprigs thyme	8 teaspoons olive oil

In a stockpot, sweat the tomatoes, carrots, leek, shallots, and garlic in the olive oil over low heat until they give off their liquid. Add the thyme, bay leaves, tomato paste, stock, salt, and pepper. Simmer, partially covered, for 20 minutes.

Remove and discard the bay leaves and thyme. Puree. Reheat the soup.

In a processor or blender, puree the basil with the oil to make a smooth paste.

Serve hot or cold with a teaspoon of the basil mixture in each serving.

YIELD: 24 servings

Soupe aux Tomates I
(Fresh Tomato Soup I)

4 onions, thinly sliced	1 cup flour
4 teaspoons minced dill	4 quarts chicken stock
4 teaspoons minced thyme	2 tablespoons sugar
4 teaspoons minced basil	salt and pepper, to taste
½ cup butter	1 quart heavy cream
½ cup olive oil	2 cups grated Parmesan cheese
32 tomatoes, peeled, seeded,	grated Parmesan cheese, to
and chopped	garnish
¾ cup tomato paste	

In a stockpot, sweat the onion, dill, thyme, and basil in the butter and oil until the onion is soft. Add the tomatoes and tomato paste, and simmer 10 minutes.

In a bowl, mix the flour with 2 cups chicken stock, and stir into the soup with the remaining stock. Add sugar, salt, and pepper to taste. Simmer, stirring often, for 25 minutes.

Whip the cream until stiff, and fold in the 2 cups grated Parmesan cheese.

Serve the soup with a dollop of cream on top and additional cheese on the side.

YIELD: 24 servings

NOTE: If desired, the cups of soup can be put under the broiler to brown the cream topping before serving.

Soupe aux Tomates II
(Fresh Tomato Soup II)

8 leeks, thinly sliced	4 bay leaves
1 cup olive oil	1 tablespoon thyme
6 tablespoons flour	4 garlic cloves, crushed
2 quarts chicken or beef stock	salt and pepper, to taste
24 tomatoes, peeled, seeded, and chopped	8 quarts hot water
4 sprigs of parsley	24 to 48 croutes sautéed in olive oil
4 sprigs of celery leaves	

In a stockpot, sweat the leeks in the oil until soft and just starting to turn golden.

Sprinkle with the flour and mix well. Gradually stir in the stock and bring to a boil.

Add the tomatoes. Make a faggot of the parsley, celery, and bay leaves, and add to the soup with the thyme, garlic, salt, and pepper. Add the hot water, cover, and simmer for 1½ hours. Remove the faggot from the soup and discard.

To serve, place 1 or 2 croutes in each plate and ladle on the soup.
YIELD: 24 servings

NOTE: If desired, serve the soup with a bowl of grated Gruyère on
the side.

Tomato Saffron Soup

2 leeks, chopped	1 teaspoon powdered saffron
2 cups carrots, chopped	5 quarts beef or chicken
1⅓ cups celery, chopped	stock
½ cup butter	salt and pepper, to taste
24 tomatoes, peeled, seeded, and chopped	4 lemons, thinly sliced and seeded, to garnish
2 tablespoons grated lemon rind	¼ cup minced parsley, to garnish

In a stockpot, sweat the leeks, carrots, and celery in the butter until
soft. Add the tomatoes, grated lemon rind, saffron, stock, and salt,
and simmer, partially covered, for 30 minutes.

Puree the soup, and return to the kettle and reheat. Correct the
seasoning with salt and pepper.

Dust one side of each lemon slice with parsley and float on the
soup.

YIELD: 24 servings

Walnut Soup

½ cup butter	¼ teaspoon Worcestershire
½ cup flour	sauce
6 quarts beef stock	Tabasco, to taste
6 cups finely ground walnuts	2 cups walnut halves, to
salt and pepper, to taste	garnish

In a stockpot, melt the butter, stir in the flour, and cook, stirring, until the roux turns golden. Stir in the stock and cook, stirring, until thickened and smooth. Add the walnuts, salt, pepper, Worcestershire sauce, and Tabasco, and simmer 30 minutes.

Serve hot, garnished with the walnut halves.

YIELD: 24 servings

Sopa de Media Hora
(Half-hour Zucchini Soup)

24 small zucchini, sliced	2 bay leaves
4 large onions, chopped	8 quarts chicken stock
2 pounds carrots, sliced	salt and pepper, to taste
8 tomatoes, peeled, seeded,	3 avocados, peeled and cut
and chopped	into strips, to garnish

In a stockpot, simmer the zucchini, onions, carrots, tomatoes, bay leaves, and chicken stock until the vegetables are tender, about 30 minutes. Correct the seasoning with salt and pepper. Remove and discard the bay leaves.

Serve garnished with the avocado strips.

YIELD: 24 servings

❧ FISH SOUPS ❧

Many diners would choose a perfectly made fish soup over any other kind of soup. From the richly subtle cream soup known as Billi Bi, to the fabulous Provençale Soupe de Poisson which serves as the base for Bouillabaisse, to the chowders so expected in New England and indeed in any fish house in the United States, these soups appeal to the appetite and often to the eye of the consumer. Without question, they can make the reputation and easily the profits of a fine restaurant.

Some fish soups, Bouillabaisse, for example, can easily escalate food costs out of control; others however can be prepared for pennies using the bones of fish that might otherwise be discarded.

In reading through this chapter, you may get the impression that many of the soups are the same. But, in fact, each has its different and distinctive flavor. It is worth your time to sample all of them. The soups for the most part come from Southern Europe, with a smattering of recipes from the Orient.

Soupe de Poisson I
(Provençal Fish Soup I)

1 quart sliced onions
1 quart sliced leeks
2 cups olive oil
6 pounds tomatoes, chopped
2 heads garlic, crushed
1 bunch parsley
2 teaspoons dried thyme
2 teaspoons fennel seeds
2 teaspoons crumbled saffron
2 teaspoons dried orange peel

16 pounds fish bones and
    trimmings (see Note)
10 quarts cold water
salt, to taste
Accompaniments:
croutons
rouille (see recipe, below)
grated Gruyère cheese

In a stockpot, sweat the onions and leeks in the oil until tender but not brown. Stir in the tomatoes and garlic, and sweat the tomatoes until the liquid begins to run. Add the parsley, thyme, fennel seeds, saffron, orange peel, fish trimmings, water, and salt. Simmer, uncovered, for 30 to 40 minutes.

Strain through a colander, pressing heavily on the ingredients to extract the flavors. Discard the contents of the strainer.

Strain again through a sieve, pressing on any ingredients to extract the flavors. Discard the contents of the sieve.

Strain again through a sieve, pressing on any remaining ingredients to extract as much flavor as possible.

To serve, pass the soup with bowls of rouille, croutons, and cheese. Each diner selects a portion of each.

YIELD: about 24 servings

NOTE: This ranks among the great soups of the world. It is nothing more than flavored fish stock, but what flavor. It will cost you little to use the trimmings from whatever fish you have on hand, though salmon and too many oily fish will change the flavor. Fish trimmings include the heads and bodies of white fish such as haddock, sole, cod, cusk, monkfish, and tile fish. They can also include shrimp shells and lobster bodies.

One of the joys of this soup is that if you decide that you want a fish soup slightly different from Bouillabaisse, just add the fish of your choice to the broth and cook until done. Serve it with the croutons and rouille.

Rouille

8 garlic cloves	1½ cups olive oil
8 red peppers, peeled	Tabasco, to taste
8 egg yolks	salt and pepper, to taste

In a processor, puree the garlic and peppers. Add the egg yolks and, with the machine running, add the oil in a slow, steady stream. Correct the seasoning with Tabasco, salt, and pepper.
YIELD: about 6 cups

Soupe de Poisson II
(Provençal Fish Soup II)

1 quart minced onions	2 teaspoons fennel seeds
1 cup olive oil	16 large tomatoes, peeled
2 pounds snapper, perch, cod, or black bass, cut into 2-inch cubes	cold water as needed
	2 teaspoons saffron, crumbled
8 garlic cloves, minced	salt and pepper, to taste
2 teaspoons thyme	garlic croutons, to accompany

In a stockpot, sweat the onions in the oil until soft. Turn up the heat and add the fish, garlic, thyme, fennel seeds, and tomatoes. Cover and boil for 20 minutes, stirring often.

Add cold water to come twice as high as the depth of the fish and boil rapidly for 20 minutes.

Force through a food mill and press through a fine sieve, extracting all of the juices.

Dissolve the saffron in a little soup and add to the soup. Reheat the soup, and correct the seasoning with salt and pepper. Serve with croutons.

YIELD: 24 servings

NOTE: This can be served with rouille (see preceding recipe) and grated Gruyère cheese, if desired.

Soupe de Poisson aux Vermicelle et Pernod
_____(Fish Soup with Vermicelli and Pernod)_____

4 quarts minced onions	1½ cups tomato paste
1 quart minced celery	4 bay leaves
1 quart minced leeks	1 cup minced parsley
½ cup minced garlic	½ cup minced thyme
1 cup olive oil	salt and pepper, to taste
4 teaspoons crumbled saffron	3 cups vermicelli, broken
12 pounds fish bones	½ cup Pernod
10 cups drained canned tomatoes	1 cup minced basil, to garnish
1 quart white wine	

In a stockpot, sweat the onion, celery, leeks, and garlic in the oil until soft. Add the saffron, fish bones, tomatoes, wine, tomato paste, bay leaves, parsley, thyme, and salt and pepper to taste. Simmer over moderately high heat for 20 minutes.

Strain, pressing out the liquid, and discard the solids. Bring the soup to a boil, add the noodles, and simmer until noodles are tender. Add the Pernod and serve in bowls sprinkled with basil.

YIELD: 24 servings

NOTE: Can be served with croutons and/or grated Gruyère cheese.

Soupe aux Poissons
_____(Soup with Fish)_____

¾ cup minced shallots
1⅓ cups olive oil
12 garlic cloves, minced
2 cups minced parsley
4 tablespoons crushed
  saffron
3 quarts tomato puree
3½ quarts fish stock
1 quart dry white wine
4 teaspoons crushed dried
  mint
4 teaspoons crushed dried
  basil

salt and pepper, to taste
cayenne pepper, to taste
2 pounds scallops
48 medium shrimp, deveined
4 pounds cod, cut into 24
  pieces
12 small lobsters, quartered
48 littleneck clams
½ cup Pernod
  croutons (optional)

In a stockpot, sweat the shallots in the oil until soft. Add the garlic and sweat until soft. Stir in the parsley, saffron, tomato puree, fish stock, wine, mint, basil, salt, pepper, and cayenne to taste. Boil rapidly for 15 minutes.

Add the scallops, shrimp, cod, and lobster, and boil over high heat for 10 minutes. Add the clams and simmer until they open. Stir in the Pernod. Pass croutons, if desired.

YIELD: 24 servings

Bouillabaisse
(Mediterranean Fish Soup)

There are dozens of versions of this world-famous soup. In France the soup must have rascasse, a rather ugly-looking fish, to be a true Bouillabaisse. Since this fish is unavailable in the United States, many versions exist that omit it. Purists insist that such versions be called Bouillabaisse Americaine or Soupe aux Poissons.

8 leeks, chopped	salt and pepper, to taste
4 onions, chopped	3 lobsters, quartered
4 carrots, chopped	4 pounds eel
2 cups olive oil	2 cups tomato juice
4 pounds tomatoes, peeled and seeded	8 quarts water
	5 pounds striped bass, cut up
12 garlic cloves, crushed	5 pounds sea bass, cut up
½ cup minced parsley	8 pounds Spanish mackerel, cut up
4 teaspoons saffron, crumbled	8 pounds red snapper, cut up
4 bay leaves	8 dozen hard-shell clams, scrubbed
1 tablespoon dried thyme	
1 tablespoon fennel	8 dozen mussels, scrubbed

In a stockpot, sweat the leeks, onions, and carrots in the oil until soft. Add the tomatoes, garlic, parsley, saffron, bay leaves, thyme, fennel, and salt and pepper to taste. Arrange the lobster and eel on top of the vegetables, and add the tomato juice and water. Bring to a full boil.

Add the bass, mackerel, and snapper, and boil hard for 10 minutes.

Add the clams and mussels, and cook until their shells open. Correct the seasoning with salt and pepper.

Serve in bowls with a mixture of the fish.

YIELD: 24 servings

NOTE: This truly is best when the fish are freshly cooked. For hotel service, it is recommended that you make the tomato base without the lobster and eel, and boil a portion at a time as orders are placed.

Broeto
(Venetian Fish Soup)

4 quarts water
8 pounds mixed small fish
   (see Note)
8 tomatoes, chopped
2 lemons, halved
4 pounds whole striped bass,
   gutted
4 pounds whole red snapper,
   gutted

½ cup butter
¾ cup olive oil
4 garlic cloves, crushed
   salt, to taste
   croutons sautéed in oil, to
     garnish
¼ cup minced parsley, to
     garnish

Bring the water to a boil, and add the small fish with the tomatoes and lemons. Simmer 30 minutes.

Remove the fish from the soup. Remove any bones from the fish, and puree. Strain the broth, and combine it with the fish puree.

Poach the bass and snapper in the broth until just cooked. Remove from the pot, and remove the bones from the fish. Cut the fish into large pieces.

In a skillet, heat the butter and oil, and sauté the garlic until it just starts to turn golden. Remove and discard the garlic.

Sauté the fish pieces in the oil until lightly colored on both sides.

Add the fish and the garlic oil to the soup. Simmer for 5 minutes. Correct seasoning with salt.

Serve in deep dishes with croutons and a sprinkling of parsley.
YIELD: 24 servings

NOTE: For small fish, gut butterfish, smelts, or small flounder.

Cacciucco
_____(Italian Fish Soup)_____

4 lobsters
2 pounds sole or halibut
4 pounds sea bass
2 cups olive oil
8 garlic cloves, minced
¼ cup minced parsley
5 teaspoons salt
½ teaspoon crushed red
   pepper

½ teaspoon sage
3 cups dry white wine
½ cup tomato paste
4 quarts clam juice or fish
   stock
2 pounds of scallops
   Italian bread, to
   accompany

Cut the lobster and fish into bite-sized pieces.

In a stockpot, heat the oil and sweat the garlic and parsley. Add the lobster, salt, red pepper, and sage. Cover and cook over low heat for 5 minutes.

Add the wine and bring to a boil. Stir in the tomato paste, clam juice, fish, and scallops. Simmer for 5 minutes or until the fish is just cooked. Correct the seasoning.

Serve in deep plates with Italian bread to soak up the juices.

YIELD: 16 servings

Cioppino
(American Fish Soup)

Despite its Italian-sounding name, this soup is a specialty of the San Francisco area, where it was created.

1 quart chopped onion
1 quart chopped green
   pepper
8 cloves garlic, minced
2 cups olive oil
16 tomatoes, peeled, seeded,
   and chopped
½ cup tomato paste
2 quarts dry white wine
2 cups minced flat-leaf
   parsley

4 teaspoons salt
   pepper, to taste
12 pounds lobsters, cut up
10 pounds cod or haddock,
   cut up
4 pounds shrimp, shelled
72 littleneck clams, scrubbed
72 mussels, scrubbed

In a stockpot, sweat the onion, pepper, and garlic in the oil until soft but not brown. Add the tomatoes, tomato paste, wine, 1 cup of the minced parsley, and salt and pepper to taste. Bring to a boil, half cover, and simmer for 15 minutes.

Add the lobster, baste with the sauce, and simmer, covered, for 10 minutes.

Add the fish and simmer, covered, for 5 minutes longer or until the fish is just firm.

Add the shrimp, clams, and mussels, and simmer for 4 to 8 minutes or until they have just opened their shells.

Serve sprinkled with the remaining parsley.

YIELD: 40 servings

Fish Soup, Merano Style

3 cups chopped carrots
3 cups chopped celery
1 quart chopped onions
2 cups chopped leeks
2 cups olive oil
2 quarts dry white wine
3 quarts fish stock
½ cup minced parsley
4 cloves garlic
   salt and pepper, to taste
4 teaspoons curry powder

4 pounds cod, cut into 1½-inch cubes
2 pounds shrimp, deveined
2 pounds scallops
1 quart rice boiled for 15 minutes in 3 quarts water, drained
1 teaspoon crumbled saffron
½ cup minced chives, to garnish

In a stockpot, sweat the carrots, celery, onions, and leeks in the oil until soft. Add the wine, fish stock, parsley, garlic, and salt and pepper to taste. Simmer for 15 minutes or until the vegetables are tender.

In a bowl, mix the curry powder with ½ cup soup. Add the mixture to the soup with the fish, shrimp, scallops, and boiled rice. Cook over moderate heat for 5 minutes or until the fish is just cooked.

Stir in the saffron, and correct the seasonings with salt and pepper.

Serve garnished with the chives.

YIELD: 24 servings

Ttioro I
(Basque Fish Soup I)

2 quarts chopped onions
2⅔ cups chopped celery
　　leaves
8 cloves garlic, crushed
¾ cup butter
1 #10 can tomatoes
1 quart chicken stock
2⅔ cups dry white wine

salt, to taste
Tabasco, to taste
2 teaspoons dried thyme
1 quart minced parsley
4 pounds fish fillets, cut into
　　1-inch squares (see Note)

In a stockpot, sweat the onions, celery leaves, and garlic in the butter until tender. Add the tomatoes, chicken stock, wine, salt, Tabasco, and thyme. Simmer, uncovered, for 30 minutes.

Add the parsley and fish, and cook until the fish is just done, about 5 minutes.

YIELD: 24 servings

NOTE: Use one or more white fish, such as cod, haddock, tilefish, or monkfish.

It took about ten years of searching to find a recipe for this Basque favorite. What intrigued me in the first place was the name with the double *t*. When I finally found a recipe, the flavor made the search worthwhile.

Ttioro II
(Basque Fish Soup II)

6 pounds live lobster	4 green peppers, julienne
salted water, to cover	4 bay leaves
3 quarts chicken stock	1 teaspoon dried red pepper
8 pounds shrimp	flakes
4 bottles dry white wine	1 teaspoon dried thyme
12 onions	2 teaspoons turmeric
16 cloves	4 pounds scallops, sliced
4 pounds celery, chopped	celery leaves, chopped, to
4 red peppers, julienne	garnish

Plunge the lobsters into boiling salted water, cover, and cook 6 minutes. Remove lobster, and allow to cool. Remove meat from shells, saving shells. Dice meat and set aside.

Place lobster shells in a stockpot, and add chicken stock and shrimp. Cook until shrimp are just opaque and remove them. Allow shrimp to cool, and peel them. Return shrimp shells to pot. Add 2 bottles wine and simmer 20 minutes. Strain, discarding all shells, and return stock to the stockpot.

Cut 8 onions into thin slices, and stick the remaining onions with the cloves. Add the celery, onions, peppers, bay leaves, pepper flakes, thyme, and turmeric. Add the remaining wine, and simmer until the celery is tender, about 30 minutes.

Add the scallops, shrimp, and lobster, and bring just to a boil. Discard the clove-studded onions and the bay leaves.

Serve sprinkled with chopped celery leaves.

YIELD: 24 servings

Fish Soup in Cream

4 onions, minced
1 quart diced leeks
2 cups diced celery
1½ cups butter
2 quarts clam juice
2 quarts dry white wine
8 garlic cloves, crushed
4 bay leaves
2 teaspoons dried thyme
1 teaspoon black pepper
 Tabasco, to taste
1⅓ cups minced parsley

48 littleneck clams, scrubbed
4 pounds red snapper or sea
 bass fillets, cut into 1½-
 inch squares
3 pounds sole fillets cut into
 2½-inch squares
48 shrimp, deveined
1 quart heavy cream, scalded
 croutons, to accompany
 white pepper, to
 accompany

In a stockpot, sweat the onions, leeks, and celery in the butter until tender. Add the clam juice, wine, garlic, bay leaves, thyme, black pepper, Tabasco, and 1 cup of the parsley. Simmer, uncovered, for 5 minutes.

Add the clams, and simmer 3 minutes. Add the snapper or sea bass, and simmer 3 minutes. Add the sole and shrimp, and simmer 3 minutes longer or until the shrimp are just cooked and the clams are open. Discard the bay leaves.

Pour on the cream and swirl the pot to mix.

Ladle into shallow soup plates, and sprinkle with the remaining parsley. Serve the croutons and white pepper separately, to use as desired.

YIELD: 24 servings

New England Fish Chowder

1 pound salt pork, diced
1 quart chopped onions
2 quarts water
8 potatoes, cut in ½-inch dice
4 pounds cod or haddock, cut
   in 1-inch cubes

4 quarts milk
salt and pepper, to taste
crumbled thyme, to taste
   (optional)

In a stockpot, render the salt pork until crisp. Remove the cracklings, and reserve. Add the onions to the fat in the pot, and sauté until soft. Add the water and potatoes, and simmer until the potatoes are barely tender. Add the fish and milk, and bring to a boil. Correct the seasoning with salt, pepper, and thyme (if using). Add the cracklings.
YIELD: 24 servings

NOTE: If the salt pork throws a lot of salt, pour off fat and reserve the fat and cracklings. Clean the stockpot and proceed with the reserved fat. Butter can be substituted for salt pork. It is less salty, but you do not have the cracklings to serve as a garnish. However, some recipes do specify topping the chowder with a pat of butter.

New England Clam Chowder

1 pound salt pork, diced
2 quarts minced onions
3 cups diced potatoes
2 teaspoons dried thyme
2 quarts water
4 quarts minced chowder
   clams and their liquor
   see Note)

4 quarts milk
½ cup butter
salt and pepper, to taste

In a stockpot, render the salt pork cubes until crisp. Remove cracklings and reserve. Add the onions and cook, stirring, until the onions are soft but not brown.

Add the potatoes, thyme, and water, and simmer until the potatoes are nearly done.

Add the clams and their liquor, the milk, the butter, and the salt and pepper to taste. Simmer 10 minutes. Sprinkle with cracklings.
YIELD: 24 servings

NOTE: If salt pork throws too much salt, pour off and reserve the fat. Clean the pot and proceed with the recipe. Butter can be used in place of the salt pork.

Clam juice is sold in cans or jars and results from the broth made from steaming clams in water. Clam liquor is the liquid around freshly opened clams. It is thicker and more viscous than clam juice.

Manhattan Clam Chowder

1 quart minced onions	4 bay leaves
1 cup minced carrots	2 quarts water
1 cup minced celery	2 teaspoons dried thyme
½ pound butter	pepper, to taste
2 quarts minced chowder clams with their liquor	12 potatoes, cut in ½-inch dice
16 large tomatoes, peeled, seeded, and chopped	

In a stockpot, sweat the onions, carrots, and celery in the butter until soft.

Drain and reserve the liquor from the clams; set the clams aside. Add the clam liquor, tomatoes, bay leaves, thyme, and pepper and simmer 45 minutes. Add the potatoes and simmer until barely tender. Add the clams and cook for 2 to 3 minutes or until just heated. Remove and discard the bay leaves.
YIELD: 24 servings

Cauliflower Clam Chowder

8 carrots, diced	1 quart clam juice
4 onions, diced	2 cups dry white wine
4 celery stalks, diced	4 cauliflowers, cut into
4 shallots, minced	florets
½ cup butter	2 cups heavy cream
6 tablespoons flour	½ cup dry sherry
2½ quarts chopped clams	4 teaspoons minced parsley
with their liquor	2 teaspoons dried thyme
2 quarts water	2 teaspoons dried tarragon

In a stockpot, sweat the carrots, onions, celery, and shallots in the butter until soft. Stir in the flour and cook, stirring, for 2 minutes.

Drain and reserve the liquor from the clams; set the clams aside. Add the clam liquor, water, clam juice, and wine to the pot. Bring to a boil, add the cauliflower, and simmer 10 minutes until the florets are tender.

Stir in the clams, cream, sherry, parsley, thyme, and tarragon, and simmer 5 minutes longer.

YIELD: 24 servings

Corn and Clam Chowder

1 pound thick-sliced bacon,	¼ cup cornstarch
diced	3 quarts light cream
1 quart minced onion	2 quarts corn kernels
8 potatoes, cut in ½-inch dice	1 quart minced clams
1 quart clam juice	salt and pepper, to taste
4 bay leaves	¼ cup minced parsley, to
1 teaspoon dried thyme,	garnish
crumbled	

Créme de Concombres Glacée; Cold Orange Carrot Soup; Iced Pea and Curry Soup (Recipes appear on pages 174, 173, and 180)

Woh Mein Chinese Soup with Noodles (Recipe appears on page 161)

Consommé Saint-Quentin (Recipe appears on page 21)

Soupe aux Moules du Calvados (Recipe appears on page 121)

Soupe de Poisson (Recipe appears on page 102)

Ouliat (Recipe appears on page 86)

Three-color Delicious Soup (Recipe appears on page 138)

Soupe Maraîchère (Recipe appears on page 61)

In a stockpot, render the bacon until crisp and brown. Remove the bacon bits and drain.

Discard all but ½ cup of the bacon drippings and sauté the onion in the drippings until soft. Add the potatoes and cook, stirring, for 3 minutes. Add the clam juice, bay leaves, and thyme. Simmer until the potatoes are tender.

In a bowl, combine the cornstarch with ½ cup of the cream. Scald the remaining cream, and add it to the soup. Stir in the cornstarch mixture, and simmer 3 minutes. Add the corn, and simmer 5 minutes. Add the clams, salt, and pepper, and heat. Serve garnished with the bacon bits and parsley.

YIELD: 24 servings

Clam and Oyster Soup

36 clams with their liquor	2 cups milk
24 oysters with their liquor	1 quart light cream
1 pound mushrooms	juice of 2 lemons
½ cup butter	¾ cup dry sherry
¼ cup flour	salt and pepper, to taste

In a processor or blender, puree the clams and oysters with their liquor and the mushrooms.

In a pot, melt the butter, stir in the flour, and cook, stirring, until it starts to turn golden. Add the milk and cream, and stir until thickened and smooth. Stir in the clam-oyster mixture with the lemon juice and reheat.

Add the sherry just before serving, and correct the seasoning with salt and pepper.

YIELD: 24 servings

Creamed Crab Soup

½ cup butter	1 cup minced celery
grated rind of 4 lemons	½ cup minced scallions
¼ cup flour	¼ cup butter
¼ cup Worcestershire sauce	4 quarts scalded milk
1 teaspoon mace	1 quart scalded cream
8 hard-cooked eggs, chopped	1 cup dry sherry, or to taste
2 quarts cooked crabmeat	salt and pepper, to taste
1 cup minced mushrooms	

In a bowl, mash the butter to a paste with the lemon rind, flour, Worcestershire sauce, mace, and eggs. Mix with the crabmeat.

In a stockpot, sweat the mushrooms, celery, and scallions in the butter until soft but not brown. Stir in the milk, cream, and crabmeat paste. Heat until hot but not boiling. Correct the seasoning with the sherry and salt and pepper to taste.

YIELD: 24 servings

Partan Bree
(Scottish Crab Soup)

3 pounds lump crabmeat	2 tablespoons anchovy paste
4 quarts hot milk	salt and pepper, to taste
2 cups rice	3 cups heavy cream
2½ quarts veal or chicken stock	

Pick over the crabmeat and set half of it aside. In a stockpot, simmer the milk and rice for 25 minutes, or until the rice is tender but not mushy. Add half the crabmeat, and puree the mixture.

In a stockpot, combine the pureed soup, stock, anchovy paste, and salt and pepper to taste. Heat the soup. Add the remaining crabmeat and the heavy cream. Heat again but do not boil.

YIELD: 24 servings

Soupe aux Langoustines d'Orthez
_____(Soup with Langoustines)_____

4 pounds cooked lobster or   8 lemons
   langoustines   12 quarts water
4 pounds cod fillets   4 pounds tomatoes, peeled
8 onions, chopped   and seeded
8 carrots, peeled and sliced   4 pimentos, minced
8 potatoes, peeled and sliced   salt and pepper, to taste
4 teaspoons dried thyme   ½ pound rice
¼ cup minced parsley   8 eggs, beaten
16 cloves garlic, crushed   minced parsley, to garnish
3 cups dry white wine

Shell the lobster and dice the meat. Set the meat aside.

Put the lobster shells, cod, 2 onions, carrots, potatoes, thyme, ¼ cup parsley, garlic, wine, and 4 of the lemons, thinly sliced, into a kettle. Add 12 quarts water, and simmer 2 hours. Strain into a clean pot.

In another stockpot, stew the remaining onions, tomatoes, and pimentos with salt and pepper to taste over low heat for one hour, or until the ingredients are reduced to a pulp. Force through a sieve or food mill into the soup.

Bring the soup to a boil, add the rice, and cook until the rice is tender. Add the reserved lobster meat.

Grate the peel of the remaining lemons and set aside. Extract the juice from the lemons and, in a bowl, combine the juice of the lemons and the beaten eggs. Mix well.

Add 1 quart hot soup to the egg mixture, mix well, and return to the soup. Cook over low heat until hot.

Serve garnished with the grated lemon peel and minced parsley.
YIELD: 24 servings

NOTE: This soup comes from the Basse Pyrenees in the town of Orthez. Although langoustines are the correct seafood to use, lobster works very well.

Cotriade de Maquereaux
_____(Mackerel Stew, Breton Style)_____

¾ cup butter
¼ cup peanut oil
2 pounds mushrooms, sliced
4 shallots, minced
20 leeks, minced
8 large onions, thinly sliced
1 cup flour
3 quarts water
3 quarts dry white wine

1 bouquet garni of parsley,
   thyme, and bay leaves
   salt and pepper, to taste
12 garlic cloves, minced
2 tablespoons curry powder
   juice of 4 lemons
24 mackerel fillets, halved
24 slices French bread, toasted
   minced parsley, to garnish

In a skillet, heat half the butter and oil, and sauté the mushrooms, shallots, and leeks until tender.

In a stockpot, heat the remaining butter and oil, and sweat the onions until tender. Add the flour and cook, stirring, for 2 minutes. Add the mushroom mixture, water, wine, and bouquet garni. Season with salt and pepper and simmer, covered, for 15 minutes.

Add the garlic and curry powder blended with the lemon juice, and mix well. Add the mackerel, and simmer 15 minutes.

Transfer the fish to a hot platter. Correct the seasoning with salt and pepper, and if necessary boil down the soup to concentrate the flavor. Remove and discard the bouquet garni. Line the soup plates with bread and pour on the soup. Top with 2 mackerel pieces and sprinkle with parsley.

YIELD: 24 servings

Soupe aux Moules du Calvados
(Normandy Mussel Soup)

2 quarts thinly sliced onions
1 quart thinly sliced carrots
1 quart thinly sliced turnips
1 quart thinly sliced leeks
2 cups thinly sliced celery
2 quarts thinly sliced
   potatoes
½ pound butter
8 quarts chicken stock
20 quarts mussels, scrubbed
8 tomatoes, peeled and
   quartered

8 shallots, minced
4 bunches parsley
4 teaspoons dried thyme
2 quarts dry white wine
1 quart heavy cream
   salt and pepper, to taste
1 pound grated Parmesan
   cheese
4 heads garlic, peeled
48 croûtes, sautéed in butter,
   to accompany

In a stockpot, sweat the onions, carrots, turnips, leeks, celery, and potatoes in the butter for 20 minutes. Add the stock, and simmer for 45 minutes.

In another stockpot, bring the mussels, tomatoes, shallots, parsley, thyme, wine, and cream to a boil over high heat, covered tightly. When the shells have opened, remove the mussel mixture from the heat and let cool enough to handle. Remove and discard the shells. Strain the cooking liquid and reserve.

Add the liquid and the mussel meat to the vegetable mixture and reheat. Correct the seasoning with salt and pepper.

Puree the grated cheese and the garlic, and spread the paste on the croutons. Heat the croûtes in the oven, and serve with the soup.

YIELD: 24 to 30 servings

Mussel and Clam Cioppino

6 onions, minced	2 cups dry white wine
6 green peppers, minced	¾ cup minced parsley
12 garlic cloves, minced	¼ cup minced basil leaves
1¼ cups olive oil	6 pounds mussels, cleaned
3 quarts fish stock	72 littleneck clams, cleaned
18 tomatoes, peeled, seeded,	salt and pepper, to taste
and chopped	minced parsley, to garnish

In a large pot, sweat the onions, peppers, and garlic in the oil. Add the fish stock, tomatoes, wine, parsley, and basil. Simmer, partially covered, for 15 minutes. Add the mussels and clams and simmer, covered, for about 6 minutes, or until the shells open. Correct the seasoning with salt and pepper, and serve in heated bowls. Sprinkle each serving with minced parsley.
YIELD: 24 servings

Mussel and Scallop Soup with Saffron

12 pounds mussels, cleaned	1¼ cups flour
20 shallots, chopped	1 quart heavy cream
½ cup chopped parsley	2 teaspoons saffron boiled
4 bay leaves	in 1 cup white wine
1 teaspoon thyme	1 pound scallops
pepper, to taste	¼ cup leek, julienne
2 cups white wine	¼ cup carrot, julienne
2 cups water	¼ cup celery, julienne
3 quarts fish stock	salt and pepper, to taste
2 cups butter	

Place mussels in a stockpot with the shallots, parsley, bay leaves, thyme, pepper, wine, water, and 2 quarts of the fish stock. Cover and bring to a boil over high heat. When the shells have opened, remove the mussels. Discard the shells, and reserve the meat for another use.

Strain the broth into a pan and reduce by one-quarter. Discard the seasoning ingredients.

In another saucepan, melt 1 cup butter and stir in the flour. Cook over low heat, stirring, for 2 minutes. Add the mussel broth, stirring, and bring to a boil and simmer 15 minutes. If too thick, add more fish stock to thin. Strain through a fine sieve into a clean pot. Heat the soup, and add the cream, the saffron and wine, and the scallops.

In the remaining quart of fish stock, blanch the leeks, carrots, and celery for 2 minutes. Drain the vegetables and add them to the soup. Swirl in the remaining butter. Correct the seasoning with salt and pepper.

YIELD: 24 servings

NOTE: The mussel meat can be served as an ingredient of the soup if desired.

Soupe aux Moules et au Riz
(Mussel and Rice Soup)

8 quarts mussels, cleaned	9 quarts hot water
water to cover	1 large bouquet garni of
4 onions, thinly sliced	thyme, bay leaves, and
8 leeks, thinly sliced	parsley
⅔ cup olive oil	salt and pepper, to taste
12 tomatoes, peeled, seeded,	1½ cups rice
and chopped	1½ teaspoons saffron

Put the mussels and water to cover into a stockpot and cook, covered, over high heat until the shells open. Remove and discard the shells, reserving the meat. Strain the broth through a fine sieve.

In a stockpot, sweat the onions and leeks in the olive oil until golden. Add the tomatoes, 9 quarts of hot water, and bouquet garni, and the salt and pepper to taste. Simmer 20 minutes.

Add the rice and saffron, and simmer 20 minutes longer, until the rice is just cooked. Add the mussels and broth.

Remove and discard the bouquet garni, and serve.
YIELD: 24 servings

Oyster Soup

¾ cup minced celery
¾ cup minced onion
¼ pound butter
½ cup flour
7½ cups scalded milk

6 egg yolks
3 quarts shucked oysters
1½ cups heavy cream
½ teaspoon ground mace

In a saucepan, sweat the celery and onion in the butter until softened. Add the flour and cook, stirring, for about 5 minutes. Stir in the milk and cook, stirring, until thickened and smooth. Simmer 5 minutes longer.

In a bowl, beat the egg yolks and slowly pour in 2 cups of hot soup while stirring constantly. Return the egg yolk mixture to the soup, and reheat, stirring, without letting it come to a boil.

In another pan, heat the oysters, cream, and mace gently, just until the edges of the oysters curl. Add to soup.
YIELD: 24 servings

Oyster and Artichoke Soup

12 dozen oysters, shucked
5 cups cold water
1 pound butter
24 tiny artichokes, boiled
2 teaspoons cayenne pepper

1 teaspoon white pepper
1 teaspoon salt
2 cups minced scallions
2 quarts heavy cream

Soak the oysters in the water for 30 minutes. Strain, reserving the oysters and the water.

In a stockpot, melt the butter. Cut the artichokes into sixths, discarding the choke and any tough outer leaves, and add to the pot. Add the cayenne pepper, white pepper, salt and 3 cups of the oyster water, and boil for 3 minutes. Add the remaining oyster water, and boil 1 minute. Stir in the scallions, and gradually whisk in the cream. Add the oysters, and simmer until the edges just begin to curl.

YIELD: 24 servings

Oyster Chowder

½ pound lean salt pork, minced	water, to cover
¼ cup butter	2 quarts milk
1 quart minced onion	2 quarts light cream
2 quarts shucked oysters with their liquor	1 teaspoon thyme
2 quarts thinly sliced potatoes	salt and pepper, to taste
	oyster crackers, to accompany

In a stockpot, sauté the pork in the butter until light brown, drain, and reserve. Add the onion to the pot and cook until soft and just barely colored.

Drain the liquor from the oysters, and add it to the stockpot with the pork bits, potatoes, and just enough water to cover the potatoes. Bring to a boil and skim the scum. Simmer 20 to 25 minutes or until the potatoes are tender.

Add the milk, cream, and thyme, and correct the seasoning with salt and pepper. Add the oysters, and cook just until the edges curl.

Serve with the oyster crackers.

YIELD: 24 servings

Oyster and Corn Chowder

½ cup butter
2 cups minced onion
4 cloves garlic, minced
16 scallions, minced
1½ quarts milk
1 quart heavy cream
1 tablespoon salt

¾ teaspoon black pepper
1 quart oyster liquor
1 quart shucked oysters
2 quarts fresh corn kernels
½ cup minced chives, to
    garnish

In a stockpot, melt the butter, add the onion, garlic, and scallions, and simmer until soft. Add the milk and cream, and bring to a boil. Add the salt, pepper, oyster liquor, oysters, and corn, and bring to a boil. Turn off heat, and let chowder set 5 minutes before serving.

Serve sprinkled with chives.

YIELD: 24 servings

Oyster and Squash Soup

2½ quarts pureed squash
4 small onions, thinly
    sliced
2 quarts evaporated milk
1 quart water
½ cup butter

salt and pepper, to taste
nutmeg, to taste
1 quart light cream, scalded
2 quarts shucked oysters with
    3 cups of their liquor
large pinch paprika

In a stockpot, simmer the squash, onion, milk, water, and butter, and the salt, pepper, and nutmeg to taste, for 15 minutes.

Add the cream, drained oysters, and 3 cups oyster liquor with a large pinch of paprika. Heat just until the edges of the oysters begin to curl.

YIELD: 24 servings

Scallop Chowder

4 quarts clam broth	1 cup flour
1 cup dry white wine	2 quarts half-and-half
4 bay leaves	1 quart corn kernels
3 cups minced onions	2 pounds scallops
1 cup butter	minced parsley, to garnish

In a saucepan, simmer the broth, wine, and bay leaves for 20 minutes. Discard the bay leaves.

In a stockpot, sauté the onions in the butter until soft. Stir in the flour and cook, stirring, for 5 minutes. Stir in the half-and-half, and cook until thickened and smooth. Lower the heat, and add the hot broth. Cook, stirring occasionally, for 15 minutes.

Stir the corn into the soup, and simmer until the corn is tender, about 10 minutes.

Add the scallops, and heat until the scallops are just cooked. Serve sprinkled with parsley.

YIELD: 24 servings

Bay Scallop Chowder

12 potatoes, diced	2 pounds mushrooms, sliced
4 carrots, chopped	6 tablespoons butter
4 stalks celery, chopped	4 pounds bay scallops
4 onions	2 cups dry white wine
2 quarts chicken stock	1 quart heavy cream
2 teaspoons salt	4 egg yolks, lightly beaten
1 teaspoon pepper	½ cup minced parsley, to
2 bay leaves	garnish
2 teaspoons thyme, crumbled	paprika, to garnish

In a stockpot, simmer the potatoes, carrots, celery, onions, chicken stock, salt, pepper, bay leaves, and thyme until the vegetables are very tender. Remove and discard the bay leaves, and puree the vegetables.

In another stockpot, sauté the mushrooms in the butter until soft. Add the scallops and wine, and cook 1 minute. Stir in the cream mixed with the egg yolks, and heat.

Add the vegetable mixture, and reheat without boiling.

Serve garnished with parsley and paprika.

YIELD: 24 servings

_____Shrimp and Feta Cheese Chowder_____

4 onions, minced
4 cloves garlic, crushed
½ cup lard
8 potatoes, peeled and diced
4 tomatoes, peeled, seeded,
    and chopped
¼ cup rice
1 teaspoon crushed red
    pepper

2 teaspoons oregano
    salt and pepper, to taste
1½ quarts water,
    approximately
2 pounds shrimp, shelled
2½ quarts milk
1 cup feta cheese, crumbled

In a stockpot, sauté the onion and garlic in the lard until golden. Add the potatoes, tomatoes, rice, red pepper, oregano, salt and pepper to taste, and just enough water to cover the ingredients. Simmer, covered, for 15 minutes or until the potatoes and rice are tender.

Cut the shrimp in half lengthwise and add to the mixture with the milk. Simmer 2 minutes, and stir in the cheese.

YIELD: 24 servings

Shrimp Soup with Lemon Grass

6 quarts chicken stock
½ cup chopped dried lemon
  grass (see Note)
4 teaspoons red pepper
  flakes
  juice of 4 lemons

¼ cup *nam pla* (see Note)
6 pounds small shrimp,
  shelled
12 scallions, minced
1 bunch coriander, chopped
  (see Note)

In a stockpot, bring the stock to a boil, add the lemon grass, and simmer 5 minutes. Add the pepper flakes, lemon juice, and *nam pla*, and lower the heat. Add the shrimp and cook until just done, about 1 minute. Stir in the scallions and coriander.
YIELD: 24 servings

NOTE: *Nam Pla*, a fish sauce, and lemon grass are available in most Asian markets. Coriander, also called Chinese parsley or cilantro, can be found in Hispanic and Asian markets.

Fishball Soup

1 pound fillets of sole
½ pound ground pork
¼ cup water
¼ cup cornstarch
4 quarts chicken stock

8 scallions, minced
½ cup dry sherry
4 teaspoons salt
4 tablespoons rice vinegar

In a processor, puree the sole and pork. Add the water and cornstarch, and process until well combined. Shape the mixture into 1-inch balls.

Poach the balls in the chicken stock for 15 minutes. Be careful not to let the soup boil in the first 10 minutes of poaching. Add the scallions, sherry, salt, and vinegar. Reheat.
YIELD: 16 servings

Stuffed Flower Soup

2 cups black mushrooms	¼ cup cornstarch
1 cup peanut oil	3 tablespoons sesame oil
4 pounds scallops	2 tablespoons salt
2 cups water	pepper, to taste
½ cup sesame oil	vegetable oil, to coat pan
1 quart julienne raw pork	8 eggs, beaten with ¼ cup
4 onions, minced	milk
1 quart shredded bamboo	8 quarts chicken stock
shoots	¼ cup rice wine
2 cups shredded carrots	¼ cup rice vinegar
2 pounds minced shrimp	¼ cup sugar
2 pounds ground pork	

Soak the mushrooms in hot water for 30 minutes, drain, cut off and discard the stems. Shred the caps.

Oil four 2-quart bowls with peanut oil and set aside. If making individual servings, oil 24 custard cups.

In a small saucepan, poach the scallops in the water until just firm. Set aside.

In a wok, heat the sesame oil and stir-fry the julienned pork in batches with the onions until the meat is browned. Transfer to a bowl. Add the mushrooms, bamboo shoots, and carrots to the wok, and stir until well mixed.

Remove half of the vegetable mixture to a container, and stir into it the shrimp, ground pork, cornstarch, sesame oil, salt, and pepper to taste. Mix well.

Spread a little oil in a 10-inch skillet, or in a small crêpe pan (for individual servings), and heat to the smoking point. Remove from the heat and add ¼ of the egg mixture, or ¹⁄₂₄ of the mixture in the smaller pan for individual servings. Rotate the pan to cover the bottom, and let the eggs stand until set. Turn the egg sheet out onto a plate, then carefully place the egg sheet in one of the oiled bowls or custard cups.

Shred the scallops and place in the nested egg sheet, top with the pork julienne and shrimp mixture, and flatten to smooth. Fold the egg sheet over the top. Repeat the procedure until you have filled all the bowls or cups. Steam for 20 to 45 minutes, depending on the size.

To serve, invert the bowl or cup over a large serving dish or a soup bowl. Meanwhile, combine the remaining pork julienne, remaining vegetables, chicken stock, wine, vinegar, and sugar, and bring to a boil. Pour around the egg balls.

With a knife, cut the top of the egg sheet into 6 wedges and curl them back over the scallop filling.

YIELD: 24 servings

❧ MEAT SOUPS ❧

The soups in this chapter use meat or meat stocks. Some of the recipes, such as Pasta in Brodo, are very light and perfect for the beginning of a meal, whereas others are fully as rich and filling as anyone would want for a full meal. Obviously you will want to select the type of soup according to the needs of your clientele. In a student area, the full-meal soups can easily create a demand for your services. In a more sophisticated dining room they can be too filling.

Most of the soups cost little to make, usually much less than the fish soups. Of course, you can always make changes in the recipes, substituting one vegetable for another as availability dictates. By combining two or more soups you can have an original. Years ago, when I worked for Duck Soup in Cambridge, we did this often and found that soups with titles like Meaty Vegetarian or Weekend with the Relatives always sold out, although the titles gave no indication of the contents and no two versions were ever the same— a fact that never bothered the customers.

Pasta in Brodo
(Pasta in Broth)

2 cups soup pasta
6 to 8 quarts stock, chicken,
        beef, or veal
        grated Parmesan cheese,
        to accompany

Cook the pasta in the boiling stock until *al dente*. Serve the soup in cups, and pass the cheese separately.
YIELD: 24 servings

NOTE: Soup pasta is any tiny pasta. There are many types, with descriptive names like stars (stellae), rice (orzo), melon seeds (semi di melone), and so on. Italian cooks commonly use a mixture of beef and chicken stock to make an intermediate flavor.

Tortellini in Brodo
(Tortellini in Broth)

This is a version of the pasta recipe above, except that small tortellini or raviolini are used in place of the dried pasta. The proportions are 3 to 4 pounds of filled pasta to 6 to 8 quarts of stock.

The pasta can be filled with any minced leftovers you have available. It is time-consuming to make the little pastas, however, and it may be better for your labor costs to purchase prepared tortellini or raviolini from a reliable supplier.

Avgolemonou
(Greek Egg-Lemon Soup)

1⅓ cups rice	1 to 2 quarts heavy cream
6 quarts chicken stock	(optional)
grated rind of 4 lemons	½ cup minced dill
20 egg yolks	(optional)
juice of 8 lemons	
lemon wedges, to garnish	

In a stockpot, simmer the rice and stock for 30 minutes. Stir in the lemon rind. In a bowl, beat the egg yolks and lemon juice with 1 quart of the hot stock. Return to the soup, and cook gently until thick enough to coat the back of a spoon. Do not let the soup boil.

Serve with lemon wedges.

YIELD: 24 servings

NOTE: To serve the soup cold, puree in a blender and add the heavy cream to achieve a fluid consistency. Serve the soup with lemon wedges and minced dill.

Ginestrata
(Egg and Marsala Soup)

24 egg yolks
2 cups dry Marsala
3 quarts chicken stock
1 teaspoon cinnamon

1 cup butter, softened
1 teaspoon sugar
1 teaspoon nutmeg

In a saucepan, beat the egg yolks together. Beat in the Marsala, chicken stock, and cinnamon, and cook, stirring constantly while adding the butter very slowly in small bits.

When the soup starts to thicken but before it boils, remove from the heat.

Mix the sugar and nutmeg together, and sprinkle lightly over each serving.

YIELD: 16 servings

Stracciatella alla Romana
(Italian Egg-Drop Soup)

16 eggs
1 cup grated Parmesan cheese
8 quarts chicken stock

½ cup minced parsley, to
   garnish

In a bowl, beat the eggs and cheese together. In a pot, bring the stock to just below the boiling point. Add the egg mixture in a slow, steady stream, stirring constantly until the eggs separate into shreds. Sprinkle with parsley and serve.

YIELD: 24 servings

Zuppa alla Pavese
(Chicken Soup, Pavia Style)

24 thick slices Italian bread	10 quarts chicken stock
1 cup softened butter	salt and pepper, to taste
2 cups grated Parmesan cheese	grated Parmesan cheese, to accompany
24 eggs, at room temperature	

Butter the bread slices and coat with grated cheese. Brown under the broiler until golden. Season stock and bring to a boil.

Place a slice of bread in each soup bowl, break an egg on top, and gently pour the boiling stock over each egg. Pass additional cheese on the side.

YIELD: 24 servings

NOTE: This soup must be very hot and the eggs at room temperature. The soup should poach the egg to the point that the white is cooked and the yolk is still runny.

Chicken Corn Soup

4 broilers, cut up	pepper, to taste
10 quarts chicken stock	2 pounds egg noodles, broken
2 cups minced celery	2 quarts corn kernels
1 cup minced parsley	pinch crumbled saffron
4 teaspoons salt	

In a stockpot, simmer the chickens in the stock until tender, about 30 minutes. Remove the chicken from the stock, cut the meat into ½-inch dice, and set the meat aside.

Add to the stock the celery, parsley, salt, and pepper to taste, and bring to a boil. Add the noodles, corn, and saffron, and simmer 15 minutes or until the noodles are just cooked. Return the chicken meat to the soup, and correct the seasoning with salt and pepper.
YIELD: 24 servings

Lima Bean and Chicken Soup

4 3-pound fryers, cut up	8 potatoes, diced
6 quarts water	4 cups cooked corn kernels
16 bay leaves	2½ quarts cooked lima beans
½ cup peppercorns	4 teaspoons Worcestershire
4 teaspoons thyme	sauce
4 onions stuck with 8	1 teaspoon cayenne pepper
cloves	1 quart heavy cream
¾ cup flour	salt, to taste
1¼ cups water	½ cup minced parsley, to
2 quarts peeled, seeded,	garnish
and chopped tomatoes	

In stockpot, simmer the chickens, water, bay leaves, peppercorns, thyme, and onions, covered, for 45 minutes or until the chicken is tender. Remove the chickens, and allow them to cool. Bone the chickens, dice the meat, and set it aside.

Strain the stock, and bring to a boil. In a bowl, mix the flour and water to form a slurry, and add to the simmering soup, stirring constantly until the soup thickens.

Add the tomatoes and potatoes, and simmer, covered, for 20 minutes. Add the corn, beans, Worcestershire sauce, and cayenne pepper, and simmer for 10 minutes.

Add the diced chicken and the cream. Correct the seasoning with salt.

Serve garnished with the parsley.
YIELD: 24 servings

Minted Chicken and Pea Soup

6 quarts chicken stock
2 onions stuck with 4
 cloves
4 garlic cloves
1½ tablespoons dried
 tarragon

12 pounds green peas,
 shelled
 salt and pepper, to taste
3 quarts heavy cream
2 to 3 cups minced mint, to
 garnish

In a stockpot, simmer the chicken stock, onions, garlic, tarragon, peas, and salt and pepper to taste until the peas are tender. Puree and reheat gently.

Serve garnished with a liberal sprinkling of mint. If desired, chill and serve cold.

YIELD: 24 servings

Three-Color Delicious Soup

2 chicken breasts, boned
4 egg whites
4 cups milk
 salt, to taste
5 quarts chicken stock
4 tomatoes, peeled, seeded,
 and diced

3 cups cooked peas
¾ cup cornstarch
1 cup water
8 egg whites

In a processor, puree the chicken, egg whites, milk, and salt to taste. Put into a pastry bag fitted with a plain #6 tube.

Bring the stock to a simmer, and season with salt. Add the tomatoes and peas, and turn off the heat. Immediately start squeezing the chicken mixture into the broth, cutting it into ½-inch-long segments. The heat of the soup will cook the chicken.

In a small bowl, mix the cornstarch and water into a slurry. Stir it into the soup.

Beat the remaining egg whites lightly, and pour into the soup in a thin, steady stream.

Serve immediately.
YIELD: 24 servings

NOTE: This soup is of Chinese origin, but the colors are those of the Italian flag, with a little stretch of the imagination. Light, flavorful, and interesting, it is perfect to have before a substantial meal.

Tinola
(Philippine Chicken Soup)

8 broilers cut into 2-inch chunks	4 teaspoons minced gingerroot
2 tablespoons salt	4 onions, thinly sliced
1 cup peanut oil	8 quarts water
	4 cups spinach, shredded

Season the chicken with salt and set aside.

In a stockpot, heat ½ cup of the oil and stir-fry the gingerroot for 30 seconds. Add the onions and cook, stirring, until soft but not brown. Remove the onions and set aside.

Brown the chicken pieces, adding more oil as needed. When the chicken is well browned, add the onions and water. Simmer, partially covered, for 40 to 50 minutes or until the chicken is tender. Just before serving, stir in the spinach.

YIELD: 24 servings

NOTE: The chicken for this soup should be cut straight through the bones so that the diners chew around the bones as they eat the soup. For a more fastidious presentation, you can remove the bones from the chicken and return the meat to the soup before serving.

_____Corned Beef and Cabbage Soup_____

2 quarts milk	1 cup butter
½ cup cornstarch	2 quarts chicken stock
2 teaspoons salt	2 quarts shredded cabbage
1 teaspoon pepper	1 quart thinly sliced carrots
1 quart thinly sliced celery	1 pound soaked corned beef,
1 cup minced scallions	shredded
8 garlic cloves, minced	

In a stockpot, stir the milk into the cornstarch and season with the salt and pepper. Cook, stirring constantly, over medium heat and bring to a boil. Boil 1 minute, remove from the heat, and set aside.

In another stockpot, sweat the celery, scallions, and garlic in the butter until soft. Add the stock, cabbage, carrots, and corned beef, and simmer 20 minutes or until the vegetables are tender. Stir in the milk and heat through.

YIELD: 24 servings

_____Mexican Beef and Macaroni Soup_____

4 pounds chuck or brisket of beef	2 cups chopped celery
	2 cups diced potatoes
4 pounds beef shanks	2 pounds canned tomatoes
4 quarts cold water	¼ cup chili powder
salt and pepper, to taste	2 teaspoons ground cumin
2 cups chopped onions	3 cups sliced zucchini
2 cups chopped green peppers	2 cups elbow macaroni
2 cups sliced carrots	

In a stockpot, simmer the chuck or brisket, shanks, water, and salt and pepper to taste for about 2 hours or until the meat is barely tender. Allow to cool, and skim the fat.

Add the onions, peppers, carrots, celery, potatoes, tomatoes, chili powder, and cumin, and simmer for 1 hour or until the meat is thoroughly tender.

Remove the meat from the pot and discard the bones. Dice the meat, and return it to the soup. Add the zucchini and macaroni and cook until tender.
YIELD: 24 servings

Beef and Barley Soup

1 cup Polish or Czech dried mushrooms	½ cup minced onion
hot water to cover	4 cloves garlic, minced
6 quarts water	¾ cup butter
9 pounds short ribs of beef, cut into 2-inch pieces	2 pounds fresh mushrooms, sliced
8 marrow bones	½ cup minced parsley
½ pound carrots, diced	1½ teaspoons thyme
6 stalks celery, diced	salt and pepper, to taste
4 leeks, sliced	1½ cups pearl barley
1½ tablespoons salt	24 triangles of toast, to accompany

Soak the dried mushrooms in hot water to cover for 30 minutes. Drain, reserving the mushrooms and the liquor. Strain the liquor through a fine cloth.

In a stockpot, simmer 6 quarts water with the short ribs, marrow bones, mushrooms, mushroom liquor, carrots, celery, leeks, and salt, covered, for 2 hours. Skim off any froth as it rises.

In a skillet, sauté the onion and garlic in the butter until the onion is softened. Add the sliced fresh mushrooms, parsley, thyme, and salt and pepper to taste, and sauté for 5 minutes. Add to the soup with the barley, and cook for 30 minutes or until the barley is tender. Remove the short ribs and marrow bones. Cut the meat into 1-inch pieces and return to the soup.

Remove the marrow from the bones, and spread it over the toast. Serve the soup with the toast triangles.
YIELD: 24 servings

_____Czechoslovakian Beef and Cabbage Soup_____

8 pounds beef bones	8 quarts shredded cabbage
1 quart chopped onions	2 #10 cans tomatoes
1 quart chopped carrots	salt, to taste
½ cup garlic cloves, chopped	Tabasco, to taste
4 bay leaves	1 cup minced parsley
8 pounds short ribs of beef	lemon juice, to taste
8 teaspoons dried thyme	¾ cups sugar
1 teaspoon paprika	4 pounds sauerkraut
8 quarts water	sour cream, to accompany

Preheat the oven to 450°F. In a roasting pan, combine the beef bones, onions, carrots, garlic, bay leaves, short ribs, thyme, and paprika. Roast until the meat is browned, about 45 minutes.

Transfer the meat, bones, and vegetables to a pot, add the water, cabbage, tomatoes, and salt and Tabasco to taste. Simmer, covered, for 1½ hours. Skim off the fat.

Add the parsley, lemon juice, sugar, and sauerkraut. Simmer, uncovered, for 1 hour.

Remove the bones and short ribs from the soup, and remove the meat from the bones. Cut the meat into cubes and return to the soup. Remove and discard the bay leaves. Simmer 5 minutes longer.

Serve with sour cream.

YIELD: 32 servings

_____Beef and Potato Soup_____

8 pounds short ribs of beef	¼ cup flour
8 quarts water	2 cups light cream
8 large potatoes, diced	salt and pepper, to taste
8 onions, chopped	

In a stockpot, bring the short ribs and water to a boil, skimming the scum as it rises. Simmer, partially covered, for 2 hours. Strain the stock into another stockpot. Remove the meat from the bones, and dice. Discard the bones. Return the meat to the soup with the potatoes and onions. Simmer 20 minutes or until tender.

In a small bowl, mix the flour and cream together. Strain into the soup, stirring constantly. Simmer the soup for 10 minutes or until slightly thickened, and season to taste with salt and pepper. YIELD: 24 servings

Gulyassuppe
(Goulash Soup)

1 pound diced bacon	12 tomatoes, peeled, seeded,
8 onions, chopped	and chopped
4 teaspoons Hungarian	salt, to taste
paprika	8 potatoes, diced
2 teaspoons caraway seeds	1 cup flour
1 teaspoon marjoram	3 cups water
4 cloves garlic, crushed	12 cooked beef frankfurters
6 quarts beef stock,	lemon juice, to taste
approximately	
4 pounds beef chuck in ½-inch cubes	

In a stockpot, heat the bacon until the fat just begins to flow. Add the onions, and sauté until golden. Stir in the paprika, caraway seeds, marjoram, and garlic. Cook, stirring, for 2 to 3 minutes.

Add the beef stock, chuck, tomatoes, and salt to taste. Simmer 20 minutes or until the meat is almost tender.

Add the potatoes and more stock, if needed. Cook until the potatoes and meat are tender.

In a bowl, combine the flour with 3 cups water to make slurry. Add it to the soup in a slow stream, stirring constantly, and simmer until thickened.

If necessary, skin the frankfurters. Cut them into ¼-inch slices, and add to the soup. Simmer for 5 minutes. Correct the seasoning with lemon juice. The soup should be slightly tart. YIELD: 24 servings

NOTE: This is a soup that is found throughout Middle Europe. Our Austrian version is delicious and very similar to Hungarian and Czechoslovakian versions.

Markklosschensuppe
_____(Marrow Dumpling Soup)_____

1 pound beef marrow	½ to ¾ cup dry breadcrumbs
salt, to taste	6 quarts simmering
grated nutmeg, to taste	beef stock
4 eggs, lightly beaten	
¼ tablespoon minced parsley	

Chop the marrow finely, and stir it in a bowl with salt and nutmeg until it is light and creamy. Stir in the eggs, parsley, and enough breadcrumbs to make a firm dough. Let stand, covered, for at least 30 minutes.

Using 2 teaspoons, shape the dough into dumplings. Shortly before serving, add the dumplings to the simmering soup, and simmer for 10 to 12 minutes longer.

YIELD: 24 servings

_____ Oxtail and Noodle Soup _____

12 pounds oxtail bones	4½ quarts water
2 cups chopped scallions	4 quarts beef stock
12 stalks celery, chopped	2 cups dry red wine
6 carrots, chopped	⅓ cup tomato paste
2 tablespoons salt	4 pounds egg noodles,
1½ tablespoons thyme	boiled for 4 minutes
1½ tablespoons marjoram	salt and pepper, to taste
1½ tablespoons pepper	
¾ teaspoon crushed rosemary	

Roast the oxtail bones in a 450°F oven for 30 minutes or until well browned. Add the scallions, celery, carrot, salt, thyme, marjoram, pepper, and rosemary, and roast for 10 minutes longer.

Turn the mixture into a stockpot. Add the water to the roasting pan and bring to a boil, scraping up the browned bits. Turn the liquid into the stockpot, and add the beef stock, wine, and tomato paste. Simmer, covered, for 1½ hours or until the meat is tender.

Strain the soup into another pot. Discard the vegetables. Remove the meat from the bones and chop it. Skim the fat from the broth, and add the meat to the pot. Bring to a simmer, and add the parboiled noodles. Simmer 3 minutes longer or until just tender. Correct the seasoning with salt and pepper.

YIELD: 24 servings

Philadelphia Pepper Pot

4 pounds cooked tripe, cut into ½-inch squares
2 veal shanks
6 quarts cold water
1 large bouquet garni
1 tablespoon salt
1 tablespoon peppercorns, slightly bruised
4 onions, each stuck with 1 clove
8 potatoes, diced
2 cups beef suet
4 cups flour
1 teaspoon salt
cold water
minced parsley, to garnish

In a stockpot, simmer the tripe and veal in the water with the bouquet garni for 3 hours. After 2 hours, add the salt and peppercorns.

Remove the meat from the bones and dice. Discard the bones. Strain the broth, and return it to the stockpot with the onions and simmer 1 hour and add the potatoes, the diced tripe, and veal. Taste for seasoning and bring to a simmer.

In a bowl, mix the suet, flour, and salt with enough cold water to make a workable dough. Shape into dumplings the size of marbles. Roll the dumplings in flour to coat, and drop into the simmering soup. Cook about 10 minutes.

Serve the soup sprinkled with the parsley.
YIELD: 24 servings

Potage d'Hiver
(Winter Soup)

2 cups minced parsley	1 quart cauliflower florets
8 garlic cloves, minced	6 cups lima beans
4 large onions, sliced	2 quarts shredded cabbage
½ pound ham, minced	2 cups sliced celery
¾ cup olive oil	1 quart chopped leeks
2 teaspoons dried basil	2 quarts zucchini, sliced
2 teaspoons dried thyme	40 ounces frozen fava beans
1 #10 can tomatoes, drained and sliced	1 quart peas
¾ cup tomato paste	1 quart chopped mushrooms
4 quarts beef or chicken stock	4 pounds meatballs (see recipe, below)
8 carrots, sliced	freshly grated Parmesan cheese, to accompany
4 potatoes, chopped	

In stockpot, sauté the parsley, garlic, onions, and ham in the oil until the onion is soft but not brown. Add the basil, thyme, tomatoes, tomato paste, and stock and simmer 30 minutes. Puree.

Return to the stockpot, and add the carrots, potatoes, cauliflower, and lima beans, and cook 20 minutes. Add the cabbage, celery, leeks, zucchini, fava beans, peas, mushrooms, and meatballs. Cook until the vegetables are tender crisp.

Serve with the cheese on the side.
YIELD: 32 servings

Meatballs

4 pounds ground beef
4 eggs
¾ cup grated Parmesan
  cheese

3 tablespoons dried basil
salt and pepper, to taste

In a bowl, mix together the beef, eggs, Parmesan, basil, and salt and pepper to taste. Mix well and shape into 1-inch balls.

Poach the meatballs directly in the soup, or sauté in butter and add to the soup when ready to serve.

YIELD: 160 meatballs

NOTE: Everyone likes a good meatball recipe. This is one. Use it in soups in sizes from ½ inch to 2 inches, or use as hors d'oeuvre in 1-inch sizes. Leftovers or extras can be served with pasta or just floated in clear broth.

Minestra di Passatelli d'Urbino
(Consommé with Dumplings, Urbino Style)

4 pounds ground beef
3 pounds spinach, cooked
6 ounces beef marrow
1 quart grated Parmesan
  cheese
6 cups soft breadcrumbs
¾ cup softened butter

5 eggs
  nutmeg, to taste
  salt, to taste
8 quarts chicken or beef stock
  grated Parmesan cheese, to
  accompany

Grind the beef to a smooth paste.

Squeeze the moisture from the spinach and chop finely. Chop the marrow finely.

Mix the meat, spinach, marrow, cheese, breadcrumbs, butter,

and eggs, and work to a smooth paste. Season to taste with nutmeg and salt.

Bring the stock to a full rolling boil. Press the paste through the holes of a colander directly into the soup, and simmer 5 minutes.

Pass grated Parmesan cheese separately.

YIELD: 24 servings

NOTE: Traditionally, this is made with an implement known as a *ferro di passatelli* to produce nuggets of meat the size of a peppercorn. A colander works quite well, as does a food mill using the largest holes.

La Minestra di Esau
_____(Beef and Lentil Soup)_____

4 pounds lean ground beef	1 quart tomato sauce
4 teaspoons salt	5 quarts warm water
1 teaspoon black pepper	4 teaspoons salt,
1 cup olive oil	approximately
4 carrots, diced	3 pounds lentils
4 stalks celery, diced	4 cloves garlic, minced
2 quarts chopped onions	¼ cup minced Italian parsley

In a bowl, mix together the beef, 4 teaspoons salt, and the pepper, and shape into meatballs 1 inch in diameter.

Heat the oil on baking sheets in a 400°F oven, and bake the meatballs until just cooked. Set the meatballs aside.

Turn the oil from the baking sheets into a stockpot and sauté the carrots, celery, and onion over high heat until lightly browned. Turn the meatballs into the pot. Add the tomato sauce and simmer 5 minutes.

Add the warm water and 4 teaspoons salt, and bring to a boil. Add the lentils and simmer, covered, for 30 to 45 minutes or until the lentils are tender. Take care not to turn the lentils to mush.

Remove from the heat and add the garlic and parsley. Correct seasoning with salt.

YIELD: 24 servings

NOTE: In Italian cookery Esau, along with Ebrea, are indications of recipes of Jewish origin. Italian cookery has an entire cuisine based on the laws of Judaism, many of which have become part of the standard Italian repertoire.

Zuppa di Pomodori con Polpettine di Vitello
_____(Tomato Meatball Soup)_____

16 potatoes, sliced	6 quarts chicken stock,
5 quarts tomatoes, peeled,	approximately
seeded, and chopped	¼ cup butter
1 pound prosciutto, chopped	2 pounds ground veal
2 cups chopped onions	8 egg yolks
1 cup chopped carrots	8 slices white bread, crusts
1 cup chopped celery	removed, and soaked in
8 garlic cloves, chopped	milk
½ cup minced parsley	½ cup grated Parmesan
2 tablespoons salt	cheese
2 teaspoons pepper	1 teaspoon grated nutmeg

In a stockpot, simmer the potatoes, tomatoes, prosciutto, 1 cup of the onions, the carrots, celery, garlic, parsley, salt, pepper, and 1 quart of the stock for 1½ hours, stirring occasionally and adding more stock as needed. Puree.

In a small pan, melt the butter and sauté the remaining onions until soft but not brown. Remove from the heat, and put into a bowl together with the veal, egg yolks, bread squeezed dry, cheese, nutmeg, and salt and pepper to taste. Mix well, and shape into 1-inch balls. In a saucepan, poach the meatballs gently in the remaining stock for 20 minutes. Add to pureed soup; add more stock if desired for a thinner soup.

YIELD: 24 servings

NOTE: If the meatballs should disintegrate in poaching, break up any whole meatballs and serve the soup as is. Of course, revise the name, so the menu does not list the meatballs.

Philippine Hamburger Soup

8 onions, chopped
4 cloves garlic, crushed
½ cup butter
4 pounds ground beef
8 potatoes, cubed and
    parboiled

8 tomatoes, peeled, seeded,
    and chopped
3 quarts beef stock
salt and pepper, to taste

Sauté the onions and garlic in the butter until soft but not brown. Add the beef and brown it, stirring to break up the lumps. Add the potatoes and tomatoes, and cook, stirring, for 10 minutes.

Add beef stock and season to taste with salt and pepper. Simmer 20 minutes.

YIELD: 24 servings

Turkish Lamb Meatball Soup

4 onions, minced
¼ cup butter
4 pounds ground lamb
1 quart cooked rice
1 teaspoon cayenne pepper
    salt and pepper, to taste

1 cup minced parsley
4 quarts beef stock
1 quart white wine
    juice of 4 lemons
8 egg yolks

In a skillet, sauté the onions in the butter until soft but not brown. Put into a bowl together with the lamb, rice, cayenne, and salt and pepper to taste. Mix well, shape into 1-inch balls, and roll balls in the parsley.

Bring the stock and wine to a boil and reduce to 4 quarts.

Arrange the meatballs in a stockpot and pour the stock over them. Simmer gently for 30 minutes.

Gradually beat the lemon juice into the egg yolks and stir into the hot soup off the heat.

Spoon into bowls, and serve garnished with any remaining parsley.

YIELD: 20 servings

Turkish Lamb and Vegetable Soup

12 pounds lamb shanks, cracked	6 onions, quartered
salt and pepper, to taste	6 carrots, coarsely grated
flour	18 egg yolks
½ cup butter	1½ cups lemon juice
½ cup oil	¾ cup butter
9 quarts water	3 tablespoons sweet paprika
	½ teaspoon cayenne pepper

Season the lamb with salt and pepper and dredge with the flour.

In a skillet, heat the butter and oil until hot, and sauté the lamb shanks until golden brown. Transfer to a stockpot, add the water, onions, and carrots, and simmer for 2 hours or until the lamb is tender. Skim any froth as it rises.

Chill soup overnight. Remove the fat, heat the soup, and strain it through a colander into a pot. Discard the vegetables and remove the meat from the bones. Chop the meat and add it to the pot.

In a bowl, mix the egg yolks and lemon juice, and stir in 1 quart of the hot broth. Return to the soup. Heat the soup until hot, but do not let it boil.

In a small skillet, melt the remaining butter, stir in the paprika and cayenne, and heat until hot. Serve the soup garnished with a teaspoon of the paprika-butter mixture.

YIELD: 24 servings

Country Broccoli Soup

8 pounds broccoli	8 quarts beef stock
7 cups minced onions	1½ pounds vermicelli, broken into 2-inch pieces
4 cloves garlic, minced	salt and pepper, to taste
½ cup olive oil	
¼ cup butter	
2 pounds smoked ham, minced	

Chop the stems and florets of the broccoli separately, and set aside.

In a stockpot, sauté the onions and garlic in the oil and butter until golden. Add the ham and cook, stirring occasionally, for 5 minutes. Stir in the stock, and bring to a boil. Add the broccoli stems, and simmer, covered, for 20 minutes. Add the florets and vermicelli, and simmer until tender, about 12 minutes. Correct the seasoning with salt and pepper.

YIELD: about 30 servings

Erwtensoep
(Dutch Pea Soup)

2 quarts dried split peas	4 celery roots, diced
12 quarts water	8 leeks, chopped
4 pig's feet, split	8 onions, chopped
1 quart diced bacon	4 bay leaves
4 pounds potatoes, thinly sliced	4 pounds smoked sausage, sliced
½ cup salt	minced parsley, to garnish
4 bunches celery leaves	

Wash the peas and soak for 12 hours in the water. Boil 1 hour. Add the pig's feet, bacon, potatoes, salt, celery leaves, celery root, leeks, onions, and bay leaves. Simmer 2 hours. Remove the pig's feet and shred the meat. Set the meat aside.

Cook the soup until it is smooth and thick and the peas are tender. Discard the bay leaves, and return the meat and the sausage to the soup. Simmer 5 minutes.

Serve hot, sprinkled with the parsley.

YIELD: 30 servings

NOTE: Some say the Dutch diet is stolid, but they just give us heartwarming food. We who have spent December in Amsterdam know that a sturdy soup is a blessing. This particular version is not only delicious, but open to many variations. You can use green or yellow peas, split or whole. If desired, omit the pig's feet and use smoked ham hocks or the bone from a smoked ham. Also, if desired, omit the celery root, and add 2 pounds of carrots and 2 onions studded with 4 cloves.

Gulärtsoppa
_____(Swedish Yellow Pea Soup)_____

6 cups whole dried yellow
    peas
6 quarts boiling water
3 pounds salt pork, blanched

3 leeks, sliced
1 teaspoon ginger
salt, to taste

In a stockpot, simmer the peas and water for 1 hour. Add the pork and leeks, and simmer another hour or until the peas are very soft. Add more liquid if needed. Flavor the soup with the ginger and salt to taste.

In Sweden the pork is removed from the soup, sliced thinly, spread with mustard, and served on the side. We suggest that the pork be diced and added to the soup.

YIELD: 24 servings

Lebencsleves
_____(Hungarian Lebbens Soup)_____

2 cups flour
4 eggs
1 teaspoon salt
4 pounds potatoes, cut into
    ½-inch cubes
8 quarts beef stock
1 pound bacon, diced

4 onions, minced
4 green peppers, julienne
¼ cup paprika
4 tomatoes, peeled, seeded,
    and chopped
salt and pepper, to taste

In a bowl, combine the flour, eggs, and 1 teaspoon of salt to make a firm dough. Roll the dough very thin, and let dry for about 2 hours. It should be like stiff paper.

Simmer the potatoes in the stock for 10 minutes.

Try out the bacon in a skillet until brown and crisp. Remove the cracklings and set aside. Break the noodle dough into small chips, and sauté the onion and noodle pieces in the bacon fat over low heat for 10 minutes. Add to the soup with salt to taste, green peppers, paprika, and tomatoes. Add the cracklings, and simmer until the potatoes and noodles are cooked, about 5 minutes. Correct the seasoning with salt and pepper.

YIELD: 32 servings

Soupe Champenoise
(Harvest Soup from Champagne)

9 quarts water	3 medium cabbages, coarsely chopped
3 pounds lean slab bacon, diced	18 medium potatoes
7½ to 9 pounds smoked pork butt	9 leeks, cut into halves lengthwise
9 carrots	salt and pepper, to taste
9 small turnips	

In a stockpot, simmer the water, bacon, and pork butt for 1½ hours. Add the carrots and turnips and cook 20 minutes. Add the cabbage, potatoes, and leeks, and cook 20 minutes longer or until the vegetables are tender. Remove the pork butt, and cut into pieces. Remove the whole carrots, turnips, and potatoes, and cut into chunks. Degrease the soup, if needed. Correct the seasoning with salt, if needed, and pepper.

YIELD: 24 servings

Soupe de Mirliton
(Haitian Bacon and Squash Soup)

12 quarts water	6 mirliton or acorn
36 ½-inch pieces marrow	squash, peeled
bone	and cubed
18 carrots, quartered	⅓ cup sugar
1½ pounds slab bacon	½ teaspoon red pepper
bouquet garni of 1 table-	salt, to taste
spoon peppercorns, 1	¾ to 1¼ cups dark rum
tablespoon coriander	½ cup lime juice
seeds, 12 garlic cloves,	1 pound vermicelli,
6 stalks celery, 1 bunch	cooked
parsley, 8 sprigs thyme,	minced parsley, to
and 4 bay leaves	garnish
6 potatoes, cubed	

In a stockpot, simmer the water, marrow bones, carrots, bacon, and bouquet garni for 1½ hours. Add the potatoes, squash, sugar, pepper, and salt to taste, and simmer for 40 minutes or until the vegetables are very tender. Strain, and discard the bouquet garni.

Puree the vegetables in a food mill. Skim the fat from the broth. Mix the broth with the vegetable puree, and reheat. Stir in the rum, lime juice, and salt to taste. Divide the vermicelli among the soup bowls, pour on the soup, and sprinkle with the parsley.
YIELD: 24 servings

NOTE: If desired, the vermicelli can be broken into 1- to 2-inch pieces before cooking and added to the soup mixture. Allow the soup to simmer 10 minutes longer to cook the pasta.

_____Polish Pork and Cabbage Soup_____

½ ounce dried mushrooms
1 cup boiling water
2 pounds spareribs
    water to cover
1 tablespoon salt,
    approximately
3 pounds cabbage, shredded
2 pounds sauerkraut with
    juices

1 cup pearl barley
1 cup diced potatoes
2 onions, chopped
1 teaspoon pepper,
    approximately
1 cup diced salt pork

Soak the mushrooms in 1 cup boiling-hot water for 20 minutes.

In a large stockpot, simmer the spareribs, water to cover, and salt, skimming the scum from the surface until it no longer appears. Add the cabbage, sauerkraut with juices, barley, potatoes, mushrooms and their soaking liquid, onions, and pepper, and simmer for 1½ hours.

In a skillet, try out the salt pork until browned and crisp. Transfer the crisp bits to the soup, and simmer 1 hour longer. Discard the fat. Remove the spareribs from the soup, cut the meat from the bones, and dice it. Return the meat to the pot. Add water if the soup is too thick, and simmer 30 minutes longer. Correct the seasoning with salt and pepper.

YIELD: 24 servings

Soupe Auvergnate
_____(Soup from the Auvergne)_____

 2 small pig's heads
 9 quarts water
15 leeks, chopped
 9 carrots, chopped
 9 turnips, chopped
 9 potatoes, diced
1½ heads cabbage, chopped

1½ pounds dried lentils,
    soaked in water
    overnight
    salt and pepper, to taste
24 slices black bread, to
    garnish

In a stockpot, place the pig's heads, water, leeks, carrots, turnips, potatoes, cabbage, and drained lentils. Simmer for 2 hours or until the meat is very tender.

Remove the pig's heads from the soup. Cut off the meat, dice it, and return it to the soup. Correct the seasoning with salt and pepper.

Place a slice of black bread on the bottom of each soup plate and pour on the soup.

YIELD: 24 servings

Potage Toulousaine
(Bean and Sausage Soup from Toulouse)

3 quarts dried white beans	4 cabbages, shredded
16 quarts water	20 leeks, sliced
8 ham bones, cut up	12 carrots, sliced
salt, to taste	8 turnips, sliced
16 sweet Italian sausages	12 stalks celery sliced
1¼ cups olive oil	bouquet garni of thyme,
12 onions, chopped	bay leaves, and parsley

Soak the beans in the water for 12 hours. In a stockpot, simmer the beans, water, and ham bones for 1 to 2 hours or until the beans are tender.

Prick the sausages with a fork, and sauté in a large skillet in the oil until browned. Remove and slice. Set aside.

In the fat in the skillet, sauté the onions until golden. Add the cabbage, leeks, carrots, turnips, and celery, and sauté for 15 minutes. Add to the bean mixture with the bouquet garni and simmer 1 hour, adding more water if needed. Add the sausage slices, and simmer 5 minutes longer.

YIELD: 30 servings

_____Split Pea Soup with Marjoram and Kielbasa_____

2 pounds split peas, soaked
  overnight
1 pound kielbasa, ½-inch-
  thick slices
3 tablespoons olive oil
2 onions, chopped
4 cloves garlic, minced

4 carrots, ¼-inch dice
4 potatoes, ½-inch dice
6 quarts chicken stock
1 tablespoon marjoram
  salt and pepper, to taste
  marjoram, to garnish

Drain the peas. In a stockpot, sauté the sausage in the oil for about 3 minutes. Add the onions, garlic, and carrots, and cook, stirring, for 4 minutes.

Add the drained peas, potatoes, and chicken stock together with the marjoram and salt and pepper to taste. Simmer 1 hour and 15 minutes, or until the peas are very soft.

Serve with an additional sprinkling of marjoram on top.

YIELD: 24 servings

_____Polish Sausage Soup_____

2 cups chopped carrots
2 cups minced celery
2 cups butter
3 quarts leeks, ½-inch
  chunks
2 quarts shredded cabbage
8 quarts chicken stock
1¼ cups flour

2 quarts potatoes, ½-inch dice
2 teaspoons dried marjoram
4 pounds skinned kielbasa,
  thinly sliced
  salt and pepper, to taste
  minced parsley, to garnish
  minced dill, to garnish

In a stockpot, sweat the carrots and celery in half the butter until soft. Add the leeks and cabbage, and sauté for 10 minutes. Stir in the stock, and simmer 15 minutes.

In a saucepan, melt the rest of the butter, stir in the flour, and cook, stirring, until it starts to turn golden. Add 2 quarts of hot stock, and cook, stirring, until thickened. Add to the stockpot, and cook, stirring, until the soup returns to a boil.

Add the potatoes and marjoram, and simmer 10 minutes. Add the kielbasa, and simmer until the vegetables are tender, about 15 minutes. Correct the seasoning with salt and pepper.

Serve garnished with the parsley and dill.

YIELD: 32 servings

Spanish Sausage and Lentil Soup

4 pounds chorizo sausage	1 tablespoon minced thyme
½ cup olive oil	2 teaspoons ground cumin
1½ pounds smoked ham, minced	seed
8 onions, minced	8 quarts chicken stock
4 green peppers, minced	1 #10 can tomatoes
4 carrots, minced	2 pounds lentils
8 garlic cloves, minced	salt and pepper, to taste
4 bay leaves	1½ pounds spinach leaves, shredded

In a stockpot, cook the sausage in the oil until browned. Remove the sausage and reserve.

Drain all but ½ cup of the fat from the pot, add the ham, onions, peppers, and carrots, and cover. Sweat over low heat, stirring occasionally, for 15 minutes. Stir in the garlic, bay leaves, thyme, and cumin and cook 5 minutes longer.

Thinly slice the sausage and add to the pot with the stock, tomatoes, and lentils. Partially cover the pot, and simmer for 2 hours. Skim any fat on the surface, remove and discard the bay leaves, and season to taste with salt and pepper.

Just before serving, stir in the spinach.

YIELD: 32 generous servings

Potage Saint-Hubert
(Game Soup)

2½ cups lentils	4 pheasants, cleaned and
8 quarts water	trussed
4 onions	salt and pepper, to taste
4 leeks	½ pound butter, melted
4 sprigs thyme	2 cups heavy cream
4 bay leaves	

Rinse the lentils in cold water and place in a stockpot with the water, onions, leeks, thyme, and bay leaves, and season with salt. Simmer 1 hour or until the lentils are soft.

Preheat the oven to 350°F.

Season the pheasants with salt and pepper and brush with the butter. Roast for 30 minutes or until slightly underdone.

Cut the pheasant meat off the bones. Dice the breast fillets, and puree the remaining meat. Strain the lentils, reserving the liquid, and puree the lentils with the pheasant puree. Press the mixture through a fine sieve. Moisten the puree with lentil stock and reheat. When hot, add the cream, correct the seasoning with salt and pepper, and serve garnished with the diced breast meat.

YIELD: 24 servings

Clouds in Spring Soup

2 skinless, boneless chicken breasts	4 1-inch pieces gingerroot, minced
4 teaspoons cornstarch	6 cups watercress leaves
½ teaspoon salt	2 cups sliced mushrooms
2 teaspoons hot pepper oil	8 egg whites, lightly beaten
2 quarts boiling water	2 tablespoons salt
4 quarts chicken stock	1 teaspoon sesame oil

Cut the chicken into slices 1½ inches long, ½ inch wide, and ¼ inch thick.

In a bowl, mix the chicken, cornstarch, salt, and oil together and let stand 5 minutes.

Add the chicken mixture to the boiling water, cook 1 minute, and drain.

In a stockpot, combine the chicken stock, chicken, gingerroot, watercress, and mushrooms. Bring to a boil and remove from the heat. Stir in the egg whites in a slow, steady stream, stirring constantly. Add the salt and sesame oil.

YIELD: 16 servings

_____Woh Mein Chinese Soup with Noodles_____

8 quarts chicken stock
1 quart snow peas, shredded
1 cup sliced water chestnuts
1 pound small mushrooms, halved
2 chicken breasts, cooked and shredded
8 chicken gizzards, cooked, peeled, and sliced
4 pounds fresh Chinese noodles

1 pound shrimp, peeled
8 chicken livers, blanched and sliced
1 pound roast pork, shredded
1 quart thinly sliced abalone (optional)
12 scallions, minced, to garnish
4 teaspoons sesame oil, to garnish

In stockpot, bring the stock to a boil, and add the snow peas, water chestnuts, and mushrooms. Simmer 2 minutes. Add the chicken breasts and gizzards, and simmer 2 minutes. Add the noodles, shrimp, livers, and pork, and simmer 2 minutes. Add the abalone (if using), and remove soup from the heat.

Sprinkle each serving with the scallions and sesame oil.

YIELD: 24 servings

_____Chinese Bean Curd and Beefball Soup_____

2 cups minced scallions
  boiling water to cover
2 pounds ground beef
8 teaspoons cornstarch
  salt and pepper, to taste

4 cakes bean curd
5 quarts chicken stock
12 leaves iceberg lettuce,
  shredded

Pour enough boiling water over the scallions in a bowl to just cover.

Place the beef in another bowl with the cornstarch and salt and pepper to taste. Strain ¼ cup of liquid from the scallions, and pour over the beef. Discard the remaining liquid and scallions. Mix the meat until well combined. Crumble the bean curd and add to the beef, kneading until mixture holds together. Shape into 1-inch balls.

Heat the stock almost to a boil, add the meatballs, and simmer until they rise to the surface. Taste soup for seasoning.

Put the shredded lettuce into the serving bowls, sprinkle with pepper, and pour on the soup and meatballs.

YIELD: 20 servings

_____Chinese Meatball and Spinach Soup_____

½ pound cellophane noodles
  boiling water to cover
2 pounds ground pork
¼ cup cornstarch
2 teaspoons salt
¼ cup soy sauce

2 eggs, lightly beaten
½ cup water
2 quarts chicken stock
2 quarts water
  salt and pepper, to taste
2 quarts spinach, stripped

Soak the noodles in boiling-hot water to cover for 15 minutes. Drain, and cut into 4-inch sections. Set aside.

In a bowl, mix well the pork, cornstarch, salt, soy sauce, eggs, and ½ cup water. Shape the mixture into 1-inch balls.

Bring the chicken stock and remaining water to a simmer and add the meatballs. Simmer gently for 2 minutes. Skim any scum from the surface. Add the noodles, and simmer 2 minutes longer.

Correct the seasoning with salt and pepper. Add the spinach, and simmer 2 minutes longer.
YIELD: 16 servings

_____Chinese Stuffed Cucumber Soup_____

12 ounces Chinese mush-
   rooms, soaked and
   minced
6 pounds ground pork
½ cup minced scallions
8 eggs, lightly beaten
2 teaspoons sesame oil
3 tablespoons dry sherry
3 tablespoons minced
   coriander
2 teaspoons salt
1 teaspoon sugar

½ teaspoon white pepper
12 large cucumbers cut into
   1½-inch lengths and
   hollowed with an apple
   corer
6 quarts boiling chicken
   stock
1 cup scallion shreds, to
   garnish
minced coriander, to
   garnish

In a bowl, combine the mushrooms, pork, scallions, eggs, sesame oil, sherry, coriander, salt, sugar, and pepper. Mix well.

Stuff the cucumbers generously with the mixture, and steam 15 minutes.

Place cucumbers in a large tureen or individual bowls, and pour on the hot stock. Garnish with the scallion shreds and minced coriander.
YIELD: 24 servings

Chinese Pork and Mushroom Soup

8 pounds pork bones	1 pound lean pork, julienne
8 scallions, trimmed	salt, to taste
8 quarts water	1 cup snow peas
4 slices gingerroot	24 slivers lemon peel
16 dried Chinese mushrooms, soaked	

In a stockpot, simmer the pork bones, scallions, water, and gingerroot for 1½ hours.

Drain the mushrooms and cut into strips.

Strain the broth, add the mushrooms, pork, and salt to taste, and simmer 10 minutes. Add the snow peas, and simmer 2 minutes longer. Add the lemon peel and serve.

YIELD: 24 servings

Hot and Sour Soup

1 cup tiger lily buds	⅓ cup soy sauce
hot water	4 teaspoons dry sherry
6 quarts chicken stock	salt, to taste
1 pound raw pork, shredded	4 teaspoons sugar
2 cups shredded bamboo shoots	½ cup rice vinegar
2 cups shredded bean curd	1 teaspoon pepper
1⅓ cups dried tree ear mushrooms, soaked and shredded	6 tablespoons cornstarch
	1 cup cold water
	8 eggs, beaten
	8 teaspoons sesame oil

Soak the tiger lily buds in hot water for 30 minutes, or until soft. Discard the hard ends. Set aside.

In a stockpot, simmer the stock, pork, bamboo shoots, bean curd, and mushrooms for 10 minutes. Add the tiger lily buds, soy sauce, sherry, salt, sugar, vinegar, and pepper, and simmer for 1 minute.

In a small bowl, mix the cornstarch and water together. Add to the soup, stir, and remove the soup from the heat.

Beat the eggs lightly and pour into the soup in a thin, steady stream, stirring rapidly. Top with sesame oil and serve.

YIELD: 24 servings

____Scallop and Ham Won Tons in Saffron Stock____

8 pounds scallops, minced	½ cup rice wine
2 pounds ground pork	salt and pepper, to taste
1 pound ground ham	240 won ton skins
2 cups water chestnuts, minced	beaten egg
24 Chinese mushrooms, soaked and minced	12 quarts water
4 eggs	8 teaspoons crumbled saffron threads
1¼ cups minced shallots	8 quarts chicken stock

In a bowl, combine the scallops, pork, ham, water chestnuts, mushrooms, eggs, shallots, wine, and salt and pepper to taste. Mix well.

Place a teaspoon of the filling in the center of a won ton skin, brush the edges with beaten egg, and bring one side up to meet the other as if making a triangle. However, instead of matching the points, put them side by side. Take the bottom two points to the right and left of the filling and twist them around the flat of the triangle and pinch them together. Set out on a baking sheet while you fill the remaining skins.

Bring 12 quarts of water to a boil and simmer a batch of won tons, stirring occasionally, until the won tons float to the top and are almost transparent. Drain. Cook the remaining won tons in batches.

Dissolve the saffron in the stock, and simmer. Add the won tons and reheat.

YIELD: 24 servings

Saimin
(Chinese Pork and Shrimp Soup)

8 pounds pork bones
8 quarts water
1 cup dried shrimp
  salt, to taste
2 pounds lean pork, julienne
3 cups tiny shrimp, shelled

2 pounds Chinese egg
  noodles
  boiling salted water
1½ cups minced scallions, to
  garnish

In a stockpot, simmer the pork bones, water, and dried shrimp for 1½ hours. Strain the broth, season with salt to taste, and add the pork and raw shrimp. Bring back to a boil and turn off the heat.

Cook the noodles in boiling salted water, and add noodles to the soup.

Serve sprinkled with scallions.

YIELD: 24 servings

❧ COLD SOUPS ❧

One of the more enticing developments in public dining is the interest in cold soups. In years gone by, a few soups were served cold only during the hottest months of the year, and then they would not be seen until the next year. Today, however, the interest in lighter foods has changed the public's perception of cool soups: They are considered "refreshing" and therefore lighter and more in line with today's tastes.

This can work to the advantage of most chefs, because these soups are easy to prepare and can be made in advance and refrigerated until needed. Generally they require no last-minute effort, and give the chef no concern about curdling or becoming too strong from reduction. Of course, they should be checked frequently to make sure that they have not fermented or spoiled. Although they will keep their flavor for a day or two, this does not mean that they have an unlimited life.

The soups should be served well chilled at about 45° to 50°F. Often they are served too cold, which reduces their flavor. Let them warm up a bit before serving, if necessary, to make them cool, refreshing, and appetizing rather than cold and flavorless.

Chilling dulls the flavors of food, and it is necessary to season cold soups more emphatically. I recommend that you flavor them to taste while still warm, and then correct the seasoning with salt and pepper after chilling.

Plan to serve the soups somewhat more dramatically than you do hot soups. Serve them in ice bowls if you have them, or simply put a cup in a bed of ice inside another bowl. Large wine glasses make superb servers for cold soups. Serve the bowls on a bed of leaves, or place a small fresh flower to one side. In fine service there is always a doily between two plates.

167

The recipes here usually are served cold, however some are good hot. In previous chapters there are many soups that can also be served cold. Avgolemonou, Billi Bi, and many of the cream soups are wonderful when served cold. They may need to be thinned with a little stock, cream, or milk, however.

Almond Gazpacho

6 cups blanched almonds	½ cup wine vinegar
water, to cover	4 egg whites
4 cloves garlic	3 quarts ice water
½ cup olive oil	salt and pepper, to taste
4 teaspoons salt	12 hard-cooked eggs, minced,
20 slices white bread, crusts	to garnish
removed	

Soak the almonds in water to cover for 8 to 12 hours. Drain. Puree the almonds and garlic, adding the olive oil to keep the mixture smooth. Process until absolutely smooth. If necessary, strain the puree and reprocess any pieces that have not been pureed.

Return the soup to the processor, and add the salt, bread, vinegar, egg whites, and 1 quart of water. Process until smooth.

Pour into a bowl and add more water to thin to desired consistency. You may not need all the water indicated. Correct the seasoning with salt and pepper.

Chill and retaste for seasoning. Serve with minced egg as a garnish.
YIELD: 24 servings

Crème Normande
(Cold Curried Apple Soup)

½ cup butter	4 quarts chicken stock
4 onions, minced	8 teaspoons cornstarch
¼ cup curry powder	water as needed
8 apples, peeled, cored, and diced	3 quarts heavy cream
lemon juice, to taste	8 egg yolks
8 teaspoons flour	salt and pepper, to taste
	watercress, to garnish

In a large saucepan, melt the butter and sauté the onion until soft but not brown. Add the curry powder and 4 of the diced apples, and cook until almost soft. Mix the remaining diced apples with the lemon juice and set aside for a garnish. Stir in the flour, and cook 1 minute. Add the stock. Make a thick paste of cornstarch and water, add to the soup, and simmer, stirring, for 5 minutes.

Make a liaison with the cream and egg yolks, and add to the soup. Heat until slightly thickened. Puree the soup, and season with salt and pepper. Chill.

Add the reserved apples to the soup with the watercress leaves just before serving.

YIELD: 24 servings

Cold Avocado Soup

8 avocados, peeled and seeded	1 quart yogurt
½ cup lime juice	salt and pepper, to taste
4 quarts chicken stock	paprika, to taste
½ cup minced green chilies	

Chop the avocados and puree. Add the lime juice, stock, chilies, yogurt, and salt and pepper to taste, and process until smooth. Chill. Serve sprinkled with paprika.

YIELD: 24 servings

Avocado Senegalese Soup

4 onions, minced	4 avocados, peeled, seeded,
4 stalks celery, minced	and chopped
½ cup butter	1 quart light cream
¼ cup flour	salt and pepper, to taste
8 teaspoons curry powder	4 avocados, thinly sliced, to
4 apples, peeled, cored, and	garnish
chopped	2 cups toasted grated coconut,
4 quarts chicken stock	to garnish

In a stockpot, sweat the onion and celery in the butter until soft. Stir in the flour and curry powder, and cook, stirring, until foamy. Add the apples and 2 quarts of stock, and cook, stirring occasionally, until the apples are very soft.

Puree the soup in a processor. Add the chopped avocados and puree again. Turn the soup into a container with the remaining chicken stock and the cream. Correct the seasoning with salt and pepper. Chill.

Retaste for seasoning. Serve garnished with avocado slices and coconut.

YIELD: 24 servings

NOTE: Avocado turns dark quickly when exposed to the air. To preserve the avocado slices for garnish, toss them in lemon juice.

Russian Borscht

1 #10 can whole beets with	½ cup vinegar, approximately
juice	½ cup brown sugar,
2 cups tomato puree	approximately
4 small cabbages, shredded	8 bay leaves
2 cups diced carrots	salt and pepper, to taste
3 cups chopped onion	sour cream, to accompany
4 quarts beef stock	

Drain the beet juice and reserve. Grate the beets and mix with the beet juice and the tomato puree.

In a stockpot, mix the cabbages, carrots, onion, and stock, and bring to a boil. Add the vinegar, sugar, bay leaves, and salt and pepper to taste. Simmer, uncovered, 20 minutes. Add the beet mixture and simmer for 5 minutes. Remove and discard the bay leaves.

Correct the seasoning with vinegar and sugar to achieve a pleasant sweet-and-sour taste.

Serve hot or cold. Pass the sour cream.

YIELD: 24 servings

Simple Summer Borscht

1 #10 can whole beets with juice	4 bay leaves
2½ quarts beef stock	juice of 4 lemons
½ cup meat extract	salt and pepper, to taste
¼ cup sugar, approximately	2 quarts sour cream, to accompany

Drain the liquid from the beets, and combine with the stock and meat extract in a stockpot. Stir in the sugar and bay leaves, and bring to a boil.

Grate the beets, and stir into the soup. Simmer 4 minutes, and correct the seasoning with lemon juice and sugar to achieve a sweet-and-sour taste. Discard the bay leaves, and chill the soup. Season the soup with salt and pepper.

Serve with sour cream on the side.

YIELD: 20 servings

_____Cold Beet and Cherry Soup_____

10 pounds beets, peeled and grated	16 whole cloves
5 quarts water	juice of 4 lemons, approximately
4 pounds cherries, pitted	honey, to taste
2 quarts water	salt, to taste

In a stockpot, simmer the beets and water for 30 minutes. Strain the soup, discarding the beets.

In another stockpot, simmer the cherries in the water with the cloves for 10 minutes. Add the lemon juice and honey to taste to achieve a sweet-and-sour taste. Combine with the beet stock, and correct the seasoning with salt. Add more lemon juice or honey, if needed. Chill.

Can be served hot or cold.

YIELD: 24 servings

NOTE: If desired, serve with dollops of whipped cream seasoned with salt.

_____Jellied Beet Bouillon with Caviar_____

1 #10 can sliced beets with juice	6 tablespoons gelatin
4 quarts hot chicken or beef stock	1⅓ cups dry sherry
	¼ cup lemon juice
	¼ cup caviar, or to taste

In a stockpot, heat the beets, their juice, and the stock. Soften the gelatin in the sherry and stir into the hot soup with the lemon juice until the gelatin is dissolved. Let cool to the consistency of raw egg white.

Arrange the beet slices in the bottom of soup cups. Cover with the bouillon, garnish with the caviar, and chill until set.

YIELD: 24 servings

NOTE: For a more vibrant presentation, omit the caviar from the bowls until ready to serve. Then garnish each serving with a dollop of sour cream and place the caviar on top.

Potage Purée de Carottes et de Tomates
_____(Puree of Carrot and Tomato Soup)_____

4 pounds carrots, cooked	4 quarts chicken stock
1 quart tomato puree	salt and pepper, to taste
5 tablespoons tapioca	2 carrots, shredded

Puree the carrots and mix with the tomato puree. Simmer the tapioca in the chicken stock for 20 minutes. Stir the carrot-tomato mixture into the stock and taste for seasoning. Chill. Garnish with shredded carrots.
YIELD: 24 servings

_____Cold Orange Carrot Soup_____

2 teaspoons minced gingerroot	6 cups orange juice
	salt and pepper, to taste
4 pounds carrots, thinly sliced	24 orange slices, peeled, to garnish
2 cups sliced leeks	⅓ cup grated carrot, to garnish
½ cup butter	
3 quarts chicken stock, approximately	2 tablespoons minced mint, to garnish

In a stockpot, sweat the ginger, carrots, and leeks in the butter until soft. Add 2 quarts of stock, and simmer until the carrots are very soft, about 30 minutes.

Force the soup through a food mill or puree in a processor. Stir in the remaining stock and the orange juice. Add more stock if the soup is too thick. Correct the seasoning with salt and pepper. Chill.

Serve topped with an orange slice, a sprinkle of grated carrot, and the mint.

YIELD: 24 servings

Crème de Concombres Glacée
(Cold Cream of Cucumber Soup)

16 cucumbers	½ cup flour
4 onions, sliced	3 cups heavy cream
2 quarts water	¼ cup minced mint, to
salt and pepper, to taste	garnish

Cut the ends off the cucumbers and peel 10 of them. Set aside 2 peeled cucumbers. Slice the remaining peeled and unpeeled cucumbers, and simmer in a stockpot with the onions, 2 cups of the water, and salt and pepper to taste until soft.

In a bowl, mix the remaining water with the flour to make a slurry. Stir into the hot soup and bring to a boil. Puree the soup, strain, and discard the seeds.

Add the cream, and correct the seasoning with salt and pepper. Chill.

Cut the reserved cucumbers in half and remove the seeds. With a sharp knife, cut the cucumbers into very fine shreds. Serve the soup garnished with the cucumber shreds and mint.

YIELD: 24 servings

Cold Cucumber and Beet Soup

8 cucumbers, peeled, seeded, and shredded	6 quarts hot chicken stock
2 quarts grated cooked beets	salt and pepper, to taste
¼ cup minced parsley	1½ cups sour cream, to garnish
3 tablespoons grated onion	minced dill, to garnish

In a large container combine the cucumbers, beets, parsley, and onion, and pour on the hot chicken stock. Season to taste with salt and pepper. Chill.

Garnish each serving with a dollop of sour cream and a sprinkling of dill.

YIELD: 24 servings

Cold Cucumber Soup

8 cucumbers, peeled and seeded	4 teaspoons grated lemon rind
4 quarts chicken stock	4 teaspoons minced dill
1 quart yogurt	salt and pepper, to taste
	sprigs of dill, to garnish

Chop the cucumber, and simmer in the stock for 10 minutes. Puree.

Stir in the yogurt, lemon rind, and minced dill. Season to taste with salt and pepper. Chill.

Serve garnished with dill sprigs.

YIELD: 24 servings

NOTE: For a variation, double the amount of yogurt and add 2 tablespoons of curry powder and 2 cups of raisins. Omit the dill.

Sopa del Sol
(Spanish Cucumber Soup)

12 cucumbers, peeled and chopped	¾ cup white wine vinegar
2 cups chopped onion	salt and pepper, to taste
4 cloves garlic, minced	1 quart tomatoes, peeled, seeded, and chopped, to garnish
2 quarts chicken stock	
2 quarts sour cream	

Place the cucumbers, onion, garlic, and chicken stock in a processor and puree. Turn into a large bowl, stir in the sour cream, vinegar, and salt and pepper to taste. Chill.

Serve garnished with the tomato.

YIELD: 16 servings

Yayla Çorbası
(Cold Yogurt Cucumber Soup)

2 cups raisins	salt, to taste
water, to cover	2 teaspoons white pepper
4 hard-cooked eggs, chopped	24 ice cubes
3 quarts yogurt	1 quart ice water
2 cups light cream	¼ cup minced parsley, to
4 cucumbers, chopped	garnish
1 cup minced scallions	¼ cup minced dill, to garnish

Soak the raisins in cold water to cover while you prepare the soup.

In a bowl, mix the eggs, yogurt, cream, cucumbers, scallions, salt, and pepper. Drain the raisins, and add to the yogurt. Mix in the ice cubes and water. Chill, covered.

Serve garnished with parsley and dill.

YIELD: 24 servings

Iced Cucumber Soup

16 large cucumbers, peeled, seeded, and chopped	¼ cup lemon juice
4 onions, minced	2 quarts light cream
¾ cup butter	4 teaspoons salt
¾ cup flour	pepper, to taste
2¾ quarts chicken stock	1 cup minced parsley, to
4 teaspoons curry powder	garnish

In a stockpot, sweat the cucumber and onion in the butter until soft but not brown. Stir in the flour and cook, stirring, until foamy. Add the stock, curry powder, and lemon juice, and cook, stirring, until thickened and smooth. Simmer 10 minutes. Puree. Stir in the cream, and season with the salt and pepper to taste. Chill.

Serve sprinkled with parsley.

YIELD: 24 servings

Cold Cream of Eggplant Soup

3 cups minced onion	6 quarts chicken stock
¾ cup butter	4½ cups heavy cream
⅓ cup curry powder	salt and pepper, to taste
7½ pounds eggplant, peeled and cut into ½-inch cubes	minced parsley, to garnish

In a stockpot, sauté the onion in the butter until soft and light brown around the edges. Add the curry powder, and cook, stirring, over low heat for 5 minutes. Add the eggplant and chicken stock, and simmer, covered, for 45 minutes or until the eggplant is very soft. Puree, and strain through a fine sieve. Stir in the cream, season to taste with salt and pepper, and chill completely.

Serve garnished with the parsley.

YIELD: 32 servings

Cold Lemon Soup

4 quarts chicken stock	salt, to taste
½ cup quick-cooking tapioca	cayenne pepper, to taste
12 egg yolks	1 quart heavy cream
½ cup lemon juice	½ cup minced fresh mint, to
¼ cup grated lemon peel	garnish

In a stockpot, bring the stock to a boil, and slowly sprinkle in the tapioca. Cook rapidly for 2 to 3 minutes, lower heat, and simmer, partially covered, for 5 minutes.

Meanwhile, in a bowl, beat the egg yolks, lemon juice, lemon peel, and salt and cayenne pepper to taste, and then stir in the cream. Add some of the soup in a slow, steady stream to heat up the egg mixture, then return it to the soup. Cook over low heat, stirring, until thick enough to coat the back of a spoon.

Chill, and serve cold with a sprinkling of mint.
YIELD: 24 servings

Lettuce and Almond Soup

8 heads Boston lettuce, shredded	2 teaspoons dry mustard
1 quart finely ground almonds	2 quarts chicken stock
4 teaspoons sugar	1 to 2 quarts medium cream
2 cups sliced onions	salt and pepper, to taste

In a stockpot, simmer the lettuce, almonds, sugar, onions, mustard, and stock for 5 minutes. Puree.

Strain the puree through a fine sieve, and blend the contents of the sieve in a blender until very smooth. Add to the soup with enough cream to achieve the desired consistency. Correct the seasoning with salt and pepper. Chill.
YIELD: 24 servings

NOTE: It is important to strain out any coarse pieces of almond so that the soup will not be gritty. You may choose to strain again after adding the cream.

_____Chilled Cream of Mushroom Soup I_____

1 pound mushrooms, minced	8 egg yolks
¼ cup butter	salt and pepper, to taste
4 quarts chicken stock	minced dill, to garnish
2 cups heavy cream	lemon slices, to garnish

In a stockpot, sweat the mushrooms in the butter until soft. Add the stock and simmer 30 minutes. Puree.

Return the soup to the pot. Make a liaison with the cream and egg yolks, and add it to the soup. Do not boil the soup. Season to taste with salt and pepper. Remove from the heat and chill.

Serve garnished with minced dill and lemon slices.

YIELD: 24 servings

_____Chilled Cream of Mushroom Soup II_____

6 pounds mushrooms	4 bay leaves
4 onions, chopped	2 quarts dry vermouth
4 stalks celery, thinly sliced	½ cup olive oil
4 carrots, thinly sliced	½ cup flour
2 teaspoons white pepper	2 teaspoons dried thyme
4 teaspoons salt	2 quarts heavy cream

Stem the mushrooms and reserve the caps.

In a stockpot, simmer the stems, onions, celery, carrots, pepper, salt, bay leaves, and vermouth for 10 minutes.

Slice the mushroom caps thinly. In a stockpot, sauté the sliced mushrooms in the oil until they start to brown. Stir in the flour and thyme, and cook, stirring, for 3 minutes.

Strain the liquid from the mushroom stems, and stir into the sautéed caps. Simmer for 10 minutes, and taste for seasoning.

Chill and remove any fat from the surface. Stir in the cream.

YIELD: 24 servings

Cold Mustard Cream Soup

½ cup butter
½ cup flour
1 cup Dijon mustard, approximately
2½ quarts chicken stock
1¼ quarts light cream

¼ cup minced onion
salt and pepper, to taste
8 egg yolks
¾ cup heavy cream
minced chives, to garnish

In a stockpot, melt the butter, stir in the flour, and cook, stirring, for 2 minutes. Stir in the mustard until smooth. Add the chicken stock, light cream, onion, and salt and pepper to taste, and simmer, stirring often, for 15 minutes.

In a bowl, mix the egg yolks and heavy cream, and make a liaison with the hot soup. Strain and chill.

Correct the seasoning with salt, pepper, and additional mustard if desired.

Serve garnished with the chives.

YIELD: 24 servings

NOTE: This unusual soup is equally delicious served hot.

Iced Pea and Curry Soup

4 onions, finely sliced
1 cup peanut oil
8 teaspoons curry powder
4 teaspoons salt
2 tablespoons sugar
cayenne pepper, to taste
8 pounds fresh peas, shelled, or 80 ounces frozen
1½ quarts water

¼ cup flour
2 quarts chicken stock
½ teaspoon nutmeg
½ teaspoon mace
2 cups light cream
2 cups heavy cream
¼ cup minced chives, to garnish
¾ pound diced cooked chicken, to garnish

In a stockpot, sauté the onion in the oil until golden. Add the curry powder, salt, sugar, and cayenne. Cook over low heat, stirring occasionally, for 10 minutes.

Add the peas and 2 cups of water, cover, and cook until the peas are soft, about 15 minutes for fresh and 5 minutes for frozen. Stir in the flour, and cook, stirring, for 5 minutes. Add the stock and 1 quart of water. Stir in the nutmeg and mace and simmer 10 minutes.

Puree the soup, and strain through a sieve. Chill.

Before serving, stir in the light cream and heavy cream and garnish with the chives and chicken.

YIELD: 24 servings

Nut Sundi Soup
(Cold Peanut Soup)

3 quarts chicken stock
2 cups dried salted peanuts
2 teaspoons chili powder
   salt and pepper, to taste

1 quart milk
lemon or cucumber slices, to
   garnish

In a stockpot, simmer the stock and nuts for 5 minutes. Puree and stir in the chili powder and salt and pepper to taste.

Return to the stockpot, and add the milk. Simmer 5 minutes. Chill.

Serve garnished with lemon or cucumber slices.

YIELD: 16 servings

NOTE: This remarkably fine soup is found in the cuisines of several African countries, particularly those along the western coast. It is popular in the southern American states. Enough chili powder should be used to make it perky without leaving the guests gasping.

Cold Red Pepper Soup

2 cups chopped onion
½ cup butter
½ cup flour
2½ quarts chicken stock
1 pound roasted and peeled
    red peppers

1 quart heavy cream
salt and pepper, to taste
dill, to garnish

In a stockpot, sweat the onion in the butter until soft, stir in the flour, and cook for 3 minutes. Stir in the chicken stock, and cook, stirring, until thickened.

Add the peppers, and simmer 5 minutes. Puree. Stir in the cream, and correct the seasoning with salt and pepper. Chill.

Serve garnished with dill.

YIELD: 16 servings

NOTE: This can be used as a base for almost any vegetable soup. Use about 1 pound of the vegetable in place of the red peppers, simmer until very tender, and puree. Garnish the soups with croutons, lemon slices, cucumber slices, minced tomatoes, or some of the original vegetable.

Vichyssoise

1½ quarts diced leeks
1 quart diced onions
¼ cup butter
3 quarts diced potatoes
4 quarts hot water

salt, to taste
2 quarts hot milk
2 quarts light cream
1 quart heavy cream
minced chives, to garnish

In a stockpot, sweat the leeks and onions in the butter until soft. Add the potatoes, 4 quarts hot water, and salt to taste. Simmer, covered, for 30 minutes or until the potatoes are soft. Force through a food mill.

Return to the pot, and add the hot milk and light cream. Bring to a boil, stirring occasionally. Strain through a fine sieve, pressing as much flavor out of the solid matter as possible.

Chill. Strain again. Stir in the heavy cream and chill again.

Serve garnished with the chives.

YIELD: 32 servings

NOTE: Although many people think of vichyssoise as the ultimate French soup, it in fact was created in the United States. Louis Diat, the chef at the original New York Ritz Hotel, created it to perk waning appetites during the summer months of 1912. It is virtually unknown in France, and people who have requested it have often been served a form of carrot soup. *Vichy* in classic French cuisine refers to carrots in the same manner that *florentine* refers to spinach.

The soup can be served hot by adding the milk and cream when the potatoes are soft. This version (Soupe Bonne Femme, page 90) is not pureed.

VARIATIONS

Vichyssoise à la Ritz: Mix 1 quart of tomato juice to every 3 quarts of Vichyssoise and chill.

Vichyssoise aux Poires (Vichyssoise with Pears): Puree 20 peeled and cored ripe pears, and add to the soup with the heavy cream.

Clam Vichyssoise: Add 2 quarts minced clam and their juices with the milk and light cream.

_____Cold Potato Soup with Roquefort Cheese_____

1 quart minced leeks	2 quarts buttermilk
2 cups minced onions	1 pound Roquefort, crumbled, to garnish
1 cup butter	½ cup minced scallions, to garnish
4 quarts chicken stock	
2 quarts diced potatoes	
salt and pepper, to taste	

o

In a stockpot, sweat the leeks and onions in the butter until soft. Stir in the stock, potatoes, and salt and pepper to taste, and simmer until the potatoes are tender.

Puree, and chill. Stir in the buttermilk, and adjust the seasoning with salt and pepper.

Serve sprinkled with the Roquefort and scallions.

YIELD: 24 servings

Crème de Potiron Glacée
(Cold Cream of Pumpkin Soup)

4 onions, minced	1 teaspoon white pepper
1⅓ cups vegetable oil	1 quart light cream
1 cup flour	2 cups heavy cream, whipped,
3 quarts chicken stock	to garnish
8 pounds pureed pumpkin	2 teaspoons grated nutmeg, to
8 teaspoons ground ginger	garnish
4 teaspoons salt	

In a stockpot, sweat the onions in the oil until soft. Add the flour and cook, stirring, for 5 minutes. Add the stock, pumpkin, ginger, salt, and pepper. Cook, stirring, until the mixture comes to a boil and is smooth.

Stir in the light cream and simmer 10 minutes. Correct the seasoning with salt and white pepper. Chill.

Serve garnished with dollops of cream sprinkled with nutmeg.

YIELD: 24 servings

NOTE: Pumpkin is a fairly popular vegetable in France, but not in the usual guise of pie that is so common in the United States. This soup is truly delicious and will appeal to your guests. Because it is so good hot or cold, it is perfect for those fall days when the temperature can be variable. Check the temperature outside and serve the soup accordingly.

Cold Curried Radish Soup

4 pounds white radishes, cut
   into ½-inch pieces
3 quarts chicken stock
   salt, to taste
1 tablespoon curry powder, or
   to taste

1 quart medium cream
   salt and pepper, to taste
   minced chives for garnish

In a stockpot, simmer the radishes, chicken stock, and salt to taste for about 10 minutes or until the radishes are tender. Puree the soup, and stir in the curry powder. Transfer to a stockpot, add the cream, and simmer for 3 minutes. Correct the seasoning with the salt and pepper. Chill.

Serve garnished with the chives.

YIELD: 24 servings

Cold Salmon Bisque

1½ quarts minced onions
1½ cups butter
   3 cups minced green
      peppers
1½ quarts flaked cooked
      salmon
   6 quarts milk

1 tablespoon paprika
   salt and pepper, to taste
1½ quarts heavy cream
½ cup sherry, or to taste
   minced green peppers, to
      garnish

In a stockpot, sweat the onions in the butter until tender. Add the peppers, and sweat until tender. Stir in the salmon, and heat through. Add the milk, and bring just to a boil. Add the paprika and salt and pepper to taste.

Allow the soup to cool. Puree the mixture, and add the cream. Chill.

Just before serving, stir in just enough sherry to give a hint of flavor. Correct seasoning with salt and pepper.

Serve garnished with minced peppers.

YIELD: 24 servings

Cold Senegalese Soup

8 onions, chopped

8 stalks celery, chopped

8 apples, peeled, cored, and chopped

¾ cup butter

½ cup curry powder

1 cup flour

4 quarts chicken stock

salt, to taste

¼ teaspoon chili powder

¼ teaspoon cayenne pepper

2 quarts heavy cream

3 quarts minced cooked chicken

avocado slices, to garnish (optional)

raisins, to garnish (optional)

toasted coconut, to garnish (optional)

In a stockpot, sauté the onions, celery, and apples in the butter until soft but not brown. Add the curry powder and sauté, stirring, for 5 minutes. Add the flour and cook, stirring, for 2 minutes. Add the stock, and simmer the mixture until thickened. Season with salt, chili powder, and cayenne.

Puree the soup, then force the puree through a fine sieve. Chill. Add the cream and chicken to the soup.

Serve the soup garnished with avocado, raisins, or coconut, or any combination of them.

YIELD: 24 servings

_____Buttermilk Shrimp Soup_____

4 quarts buttermilk
4 pounds cooked shrimp,
   chopped
4 cucumbers, peeled, seeded,
   and chopped

2 cups chopped scallions
2 green peppers, minced
24 radishes, sliced
   salt and pepper, to taste
¼ cup minced dill

In a container, mix the buttermilk, shrimp, cucumbers, scallions, peppers, radishes, and salt and pepper to taste. Mix well and chill. Add the dill just before serving.

YIELD: 24 to 30 servings

_____Uncooked Tomato Soup_____

8 quarts peeled, seeded, and
   chopped tomatoes
2 cups minced onions
1 quart chicken stock
1 quart white wine
   salt, to taste

4 teaspoons sugar
4 teaspoons minced mint
4 teaspoons white pepper
   mint sprigs, to garnish

In a bowl, mix the tomatoes and onions. Let stand, covered, at room temperature for 1 hour. Puree.

Stir in the stock, wine, salt, sugar, mint, and pepper. Chill.

Serve garnished with mint sprigs.

YIELD: 32 servings

NOTE: This is worth making only with fresh, ripe, end-of-the-summer tomatoes.

_____Cold Tomato Soup I_____

4 onions, sliced
4 carrots, sliced
1⅓ cups minced parsley
8 garlic cloves, crushed
½ cup olive oil
16 tomatoes, peeled, seeded, and chopped
2 teaspoons minced fresh thyme

2 teaspoons minced fresh basil leaves
4 teaspoons salt
2 quarts chicken stock
lemon or lime wedges, to garnish

In a stockpot, sweat the onions, carrots, parsley, and garlic in the oil until soft. Puree with the tomatoes, thyme, basil, and salt. Stir in the stock and mix well. Chill.

Serve garnished with lemon or lime wedges.

YIELD: 24 servings

_____Cold Tomato Soup II_____

1 #10 can Italian tomatoes with juice
4 quarts beef stock
1½ quarts minced celery
4 garlic cloves, crushed
2 teaspoons minced basil or dill leaves
1 teaspoon dried thyme

1 teaspoon celery seed
2 teaspoons sugar
¾ teaspoon crushed red pepper flakes
salt and pepper, to taste
sour cream, to garnish
minced dill or basil, to garnish

In a stockpot, combine the tomatoes, stock, celery, garlic, basil or dill, thyme, celery seed, sugar, red pepper, and salt and pepper to taste. Simmer for 45 minutes or until the celery is very tender. Puree. Chill.

Serve with a dollop of sour cream sprinkled with minced dill or basil.

YIELD: 32 servings

Soupe de Tomates Fraîches au Pistou
_____(Cold Tomato Soup III)_____

8 carrots, sliced	4 bay leaves
4 leeks, chopped	½ cup tomato paste
8 shallots, minced	10 quarts chicken stock
8 cloves garlic, crushed	salt and pepper, to taste
8 teaspoons olive oil	1 quart basil leaves, packed
24 tomatoes, chopped	8 garlic cloves
2 teaspoons dried thyme	olive oil

In a stockpot, sweat the carrots, leeks, shallots, and garlic in the oil until soft. Add the tomatoes, thyme, bay leaves, tomato paste, and stock, and simmer 20 minutes. Discard the bay leaves.

Puree the soup, and correct the seasoning with salt and pepper. Chill.

In a blender or processor, puree the basil and garlic, adding just enough oil to make a paste as thick as mayonnaise.

Serve the soup garnished with a dollop of the basil mixture (pistou). YIELD: 24 servings

_____Cold Tomato Soup IV_____

4 onions, chopped	2 teaspoons sugar
8 shallots, minced	salt and pepper, to taste
¼ cup butter	3 cups heavy cream
24 large tomatoes, peeled, seeded, and chopped	1⅓ cups sour cream
3 cups chicken stock	juice of 4 large limes
¼ cup tomato paste	Tabasco, to taste
¼ cup minced fresh thyme	parsley sprigs, to garnish

In a stockpot, sweat the onions and shallots in the butter until soft. Stir in the tomatoes, stock, tomato paste, thyme, sugar, and salt and pepper to taste. Simmer, covered, for 20 minutes.

Puree the soup. Stir in the cream, sour cream, lime juice, and Tabasco to taste. Strain for a finer texture. Chill.

Serve garnished with the parsley sprigs.

YIELD: 24 servings

NOTE: For a tomato sorbet, freeze the soup for 2 hours, puree in a processor, and freeze again.

_____Jellied Tomato Consommé_____

3 quarts chicken stock	¾ cup lemon juice
3 quarts tomato juice	3 cups beet juice
6 cups chopped onions	salt and pepper, to taste
¾ cup chopped celery	6 tablespoons gelatin
¾ cup minced chives	½ cup water
16 garlic cloves, crushed	sour cream, to garnish
6 whole cloves	(optional)
2 tablespoons Worcestershire	heavy cream, whipped and
sauce	salted, to garnish
2 tablespoons sugar	(optional)

In a stockpot, simmer the stock, tomato juice, onions, celery, chives, garlic, cloves, Worcestershire sauce, and sugar for 45 minutes.

Stir in the lemon juice, beet juice, and salt and pepper to taste. Strain through a very fine sieve, and discard the solids.

In a small saucepan, soften the gelatin in the water and dissolve over low heat. Stir into the consommé, and chill until set.

Scoop into clear glass bowls to serve. Garnish with sour cream or whipped, salted heavy cream, if desired.

YIELD: 24 servings

NOTE: For a firm consistency, double the amount of the gelatin. Chop the "soup" with a knife.

This consommé is not crystal clear. If you wish a clear consommé, follow the directions for clarifying consommé in the introduction to the chapter on "Consommés."

Gazpacho
(Chilled Tomato Soup with Vegetables)

1½ quarts cubed white bread, toasted
¼ cup salt
2 tablespoons ground cumin
¾ cup olive oil
16 cloves garlic, crushed
3 quarts tomatoes, peeled, seeded, and chopped
3 quarts cold water
black pepper, to taste
cayenne pepper, to taste

½ to 1 cup vinegar, to taste
12 ice cubes
Accompaniments:
2 to 3 quarts sautéed croutons
8 peppers, diced
8 stalks celery, diced
4 cucumbers, seeded and diced
4 onions, diced
12 tomatoes, diced

Puree the bread, salt, cumin, oil, garlic, and tomatoes. Pour into a container, and add the cold water, pepper, cayenne, vinegar, and ice cubes. Chill.

Place the croutons, peppers, celery, cucumbers, onions, and tomatoes separately in small bowls.

Serve the soup and let the diner select from the bowls of croutons and vegetables.

YIELD: 24 servings

Green Gazpacho

8 tomatoes, peeled and chopped
12 stalks celery, chopped
4 cucumbers, peeled and chopped
1 quart chopped romaine lettuce

1 cup orange juice
4 scallions, chopped
lemon juice, to taste
minced parsley, to garnish

In a blender, puree the tomatoes, celery, cucumbers, lettuce, orange juice, scallions and lemon juice in batches. Chill.

Serve with minced parsley to garnish.
YIELD: 24 servings

White Gazpacho with Grapes

1½ quarts blanched almonds	salt, to taste
2 cups breadcrumbs, without crusts	2½ quarts ice water
1 cup milk	4 tablespoons white vinegar
⅓ cup minced garlic	1½ quarts peeled green seedless grapes, to garnish
3 cups olive oil	

Puree the almonds, breadcrumbs, milk, and garlic, and slowly add the oil. Blend for 5 minutes after the last oil is added. Season to taste with salt. Gradually add the ice water and then the vinegar.

Serve very cold, garnished with the grapes.
YIELD: 24 servings

NOTE: Peeling grapes is laborious—a lovely touch, but one you may choose to ignore.

Potage à la Freneuse
(Cold Cream of Turnip Soup)

4 pounds turnips, cut in 1-inch cubes	3 quarts heavy cream
1 cup butter	2 teaspoons Worcestershire sauce
3½ quarts chicken stock	salt and pepper, to taste
2 quarts peeled, cubed potatoes	Tabasco, to taste

In a stockpot, sweat the turnips in the butter, stirring occasionally until soft. Add the stock and potatoes, and simmer about 20 minutes.

Puree and chill. Stir in the cream, and correct the seasoning with the Worcestershire sauce and the salt, pepper, and Tabasco to taste.
YIELD: 24 servings

_____Cold Yogurt Soup with Ham and Cucumber_____

2 quarts yogurt	3 cups julienne of cooked
1 quart soda water	ham
1½ cups heavy cream	salt and pepper, to taste
3 cups julienne of cucumber	1 cup minced chives, to garnish

In a bowl, mix together the yogurt, water, and cream. Add the cucumber and ham, and season with salt and pepper to taste. Chill.
Serve garnished with the chives.
YIELD: 24 servings

_____Cold Zucchini Soup_____

8 zucchini, thinly sliced	1 quart sour cream or yogurt
4 green peppers, chopped	¼ cup minced parsley
2 cups chopped onion	2 teaspoons minced dill
3 quarts chicken stock	salt and pepper, to taste

Set aside 24 slices of zucchini for garnish.
In a stockpot, simmer the remaining zucchini with the peppers, onions, and stock for 20 minutes.
Puree. Add the sour cream or yogurt, parsley, and dill. Correct the seasoning with salt and pepper. Chill.
Serve garnished with raw zucchini slices.
YIELD: 24 servings

❧ FRUIT SOUPS ❧

Fruit soups are one of the stranger culinary treats. They are popular in Northern and Central Europe in particular, and are served as a first course, light luncheon, or in some instances as dessert. Most other cultures do not have fruit soups and often consider them unpalatable.

I have not found them to be much in demand. I suggest that you try them in small quantities before having them on the menu on a regular basis. Serve a small cup with a fruit platter for a light luncheon, and note what is returned in order to gauge the popularity of fruit soups with your clientele.

Most of these soups are quickly and easily made, but they do not last long. The fruits will ferment and create a sharp-flavored, rather unpleasant soup. Be sure to check the soup each day before serving. Use only fresh, unblemished fruits to achieve a longer life. Even a small bit of over-aged fruit can ruin the entire batch within hours.

Cold Apple and Apricot Soup

8 pounds tart apples, peeled and quartered
1 pound dried apricots
1½ quarts beef stock
4 bay leaves
8 sprigs parsley
8 stalks celery, chopped
salt and pepper, to taste
water, to cover
4 quarts milk, approximately
2 cups heavy cream, whipped, to garnish

In a stockpot, place the apples, apricots, stock, bay leaves, parsley, celery, and salt and pepper to taste with enough water to cover. Simmer, covered, for 20 to 30 minutes or until the fruit is soft. Remove and discard the bay leaves.

Puree, add the milk, and correct the seasoning with salt and pepper. Add more milk to thin to the desired consistency. Chill completely.

Serve garnished with dollops of whipped cream.

YIELD: 24 servings

Cold Fresh Fruit Soup

4 cantaloupes
4 quarts strawberries, hulled
2 pounds green seedless
   grapes
16 apples, peeled, cored, and
   chopped

3 cups lemon juice
2 cups sugar
6 quarts water
6 cups orange juice
   sour cream, to garnish

Remove pulp from cantaloupes and chop coarsely.

In a stockpot, simmer the cantaloupe, strawberries, grapes, apples, 2 cups lemon juice, sugar, and water, uncovered, for 15 minutes.

Puree, strain, and add the remaining lemon juice and the orange juice. Chill.

Serve garnished with the sour cream.

YIELD: 24 servings

Cold Blueberry Soup

1 quart blueberries, stemmed
   juice of 2 lemons
4 sticks cinnamon
2 quarts water
1 cup sugar

   salt, to taste
¼ cup cornstarch
½ cup water
1 quart heavy cream

In a stockpot, simmer the blueberries, lemon juice, cinnamon, and 2 quarts water for 10 minutes. Add the sugar and salt to taste.

In a bowl, mix the cornstarch with ½ cup water and stir into the hot soup. Cook, stirring, until the soup is thickened and clear.

Discard the cinnamon, and puree the soup. Allow soup to cool, and stir in 2 cups of the cream. Chill.

Beat the remaining 2 cups of cream until stiff and garnish each serving with a dollop.

YIELD: 16 servings

Cold Banana Soup

16 large ripe bananas, peeled	grated rind of 4 oranges
5 quarts milk	4 teaspoons cornstarch
sugar, to taste	¼ cup cold water
salt, to taste	4 bananas, to garnish

Puree the bananas and put into a pot with the milk and sugar and salt to taste. Stir in the orange rind, and bring to a boil. Mix the cornstarch with ¼ cup cold water and stir into the soup. Cook, stirring, until thickened. Chill.

Serve garnished with fresh banana slices.

YIELD: 16 servings

Soupe aux Cerises (Hot Cherry Soup)

6 pounds sour cherries	1 cup kirsch
¾ cup butter	4 pieces lemon peel
⅓ cup flour	1 quart cold water
5 quarts boiling water	24 slices French bread sautéed
½ cup sugar	in butter

Pit the cherries, and reserve both the pits and the fruit.

In a stockpot, make a roux with the butter and flour, and cook, stirring, for 4 minutes. Stir in the boiling water and bring to a boil. Add the cherries, sugar, kirsch, and lemon peel. Simmer 20 minutes, and discard the lemon peel.

In another stockpot, place the cherry pits and cold water, and simmer for 15 minutes. Strain and reserve the liquid.

Line a heated tureen or individual soup bowls with bread and pour on the strained liquid from the pits and the strained soup.
YIELD: 16 servings

Peach Soup

2 quarts pureed peaches	4 cloves
½ cup lemon juice	4 sticks cinnamon
½ cup sugar	salt, to taste
4 bottles dry white wine	sour cream, to garnish
4 bay leaves	

In a bowl, mix the pureed peaches, lemon juice, and sugar. Let stand, covered, for 20 minutes.

In a saucepan, simmer the wine, bay leaves, cloves, cinnamon sticks, and the salt to taste for 5 minutes. Strain and chill. Stir the wine into the puree and chill.

Garnish each serving with sour cream.
YIELD: 24 servings

Cold Peach Soup

36 peaches, peeled and stoned	3 quarts dry white wine
6 small navel oranges, halved	3 quarts water
3 lemons, pits removed	2 cups sugar
1 bouquet garni of 3 bay leaves, 2 2-inch pieces cinnamon stick, and 10 whole cloves	2 tablespoons cornstarch
	2¼ cups peach brandy
	1 quart plus 1 cup ginger ale

In a stockpot, simmer the peaches, oranges, lemons, bouquet garni, wine, water, and sugar for about 1 hour or until the fruits are very soft.

In a small bowl, mix the cornstarch and brandy. Stir into the peach mixture, and bring to a boil. Let cool.

Remove the orange and lemon rinds from the fruit mixture, leaving the pulp. Discard the bouquet garni. Puree the remaining mixture, and force through a fine sieve.

Freeze 6 cups of the mixture as a sorbet. Chill the rest of the soup.

To serve, stir in the ginger ale, and serve in bowls topped with a scoop of the peach sorbet.

YIELD: 24 servings

Cold Strawberry and Blueberry Soup

6 pints strawberries, hulled	4 cinnamon sticks
6 quarts blueberries, stemmed	4 cloves
6 quarts orange juice	3 bunches fresh mint sprigs
¾ cup lemon juice	1½ quarts heavy cream
⅓ cup sugar, or to taste	mint sprigs, to garnish

Set aside 24 strawberries and 1½ cups blueberries to garnish.

Cut the remaining strawberries in half. In a stockpot, combine the strawberries, blueberries, orange juice, lemon juice, and sugar.

Make a bouquet garni out of the cinnamon sticks, cloves, and mint sprigs, and add to the pot. Simmer 5 to 8 minutes, or until the fruit is quite soft. Allow to cool. Remove and discard the bouquet garni. Refrigerate overnight, covered.

Stir 1 quart of cream into the chilled soup. Taste for seasoning, and adjust with sugar and lemon juice to make a not-too-sweet, not-too-sour flavor.

Ladle the soup into chilled bowls. Whip the remaining cream to firm peaks, and put a dollop on each serving. Garnish with strawberries, blueberries, and mint sprigs.

YIELD: 24 servings

INDEX

Vermicelle, Soupe de Poisson aux, et Pernod, 104
Vermicelli
Fish Soup with, and Pernod, 104
Leek and, Soup, 80
Vichyssoise, 182–83
Vitello, Polpettine di, Zuppa di Pomodori con, 149
Volaille
Fonds de Crème de, 44–45
Velouté de, 44–45

Walnut Soup, 99
Watercress, Cream of Leek and, Soup, 38–39
Winter Soup, 146
Woh Mein Chinese Soup with Noodles, 161

Won Tons, Scallop and Ham, in Saffron Stock, 165

Yayla Corbasi, 176
Yogurt
Cucumber Soup, Cold, 176
Soup, Cold, with Ham and Cucumber, 193

Zöldbableves, 67
Zucchini
Soup, Cold, 193
Soup, Half-hour, 99
Zuppa
alla Pavese, 136
di Pomodori con Polpettine di Vitello, 149
di Scarola alla Siciliana, 77
Zweibelcreme Suppe, 89